Blissfully Human

An Awakening Story

Gordon Mahlon Straszheim

outskirts
press

Table of Contents

Author's Note

THE FOLLOWING MANUSCRIPT was written in two parts and is presented accordingly. It is the story of a "spiritual awakening", as uniquely expressed in the life of an individual human being... that would be me. Part One primarily covers the two-year period from the beginning of 2018 through the end of 2019. It includes the activation and awakening of the physical and energetic bodies, the emergence of expanded consciousness within, and the establishment of numerous "mystical" connections. At the end of that span, having reached a climactic point, the text of Part One poured out of me in a continuous flurry. I considered it complete... lived and documented. It is adequately labeled "Awakening."

Part Two of this book resumes the unfolding narrative, covering the entirety of 2020 and the first half of 2021. The journey reached another profound inflection point and the text of Part Two would relentlessly issue forth until finished. I have labeled this Part "Embodiment." It primarily addresses the further expansion of consciousness, divine communion, and the integration of vast divine energies to be lived into the world.

The majority of this narrative has been pulled from concurrent journal entries, both supporting its accuracy and preserving the real-time manner in which the events were experienced. For that same reason, other than a few clarifying edits, I left the first part alone, even though I would surely express it differently having lived the second part of the book. I'll let the original introduction stand for itself. Happy reading... brother g

PART ONE
AWAKENING

Introduction

OK… IF I'M going to write a book, we're going to have to say a few words about words. Words are symbols, and are designed to point to something beyond them. Not to diminish their vital importance and usefulness, but they are not as important as the truth they aim to portray. In the practical order of life, words are generally adequate to convey concrete things and ideas, but in some areas they are simply not. Feelings and sensations, for example, are very challenging to describe, as well as more ambiguous concepts such as the general subject of this book: Spirituality. Boom! That's a whopper of a word right out of the gate. This word has been widely used and applied around the world, and has been sufficiently mainstreamed in society so as to not set off any major alarms. Its meaning and use are wide ranging depending upon context, which includes a vast array of religious and philosophical teachings and traditions. Most generally, it can be described as the basic human search for happiness. More pointedly, it refers to the human being's inward journey to discover the truth about life and the nature of their being. Finally, if you find yourself reading a book like this, you have likely already discovered that everything in life is "spiritual" anyway, with no exceptions. Spirituality… I'm going to allow it!

I'm calling this work "An Awakening Story," so we must deal with this phrase as well. First of all, it's a story… just a story. It's not a system, method, technique, or practice, but rather a particular expression of the general theme of awakening that we are all living out in our own unique way. Obviously, I'm going with the word awakening here, rather than a multitude of other words or phrases I could have employed. In general, most words surrounding this topic are so loaded and rich with cultural content that they can sometimes pull one farther away from the basic truth they are meant to convey. They can be pulled from a variety of spiritual models, and include ascension, realization, enlightenment, Christ consciousness, and many more. In no way do I devalue these words or their appropriateness in the discussion, and will likely scatter a few of them around these very pages. So, "awakening" it is. A nice general term familiar to all, for we all awaken from one world into another every morning when we open our eyes. However, in the context of a spiritual awakening, all notion of waking up or out or away from must be abandoned. This is an inner journey. While you may ultimately discover that the sacred, infinite place inside opens back up and out and away, the movement of awakening is ever inward.

Within the context of a spiritual awakening may emerge what we will call an energetic awakening. This is a process whereby the energetic or "light" body awakens and activates in the human being. The physical body is radically transformed in conjunction with the changes in the energetic body, to be able to vibrate at higher frequencies and therefore embody more expansive energy and consciousness. The majority of this narrative will focus on the time period surrounding the energetic aspect of my unfolding awakening story. A final, yet key point must be made with regard to the word awakening. It's all about the "-ing." The story is forever ongoing, happening, moving, changing, and unfolding… always in progress. There is no fixed destination, end point, or place to which you have arrived or completed your journey.

There is one more word to address before we forge ahead… "Mystical." I'm going to allow it. I'm going to need it! For when the energetic/light body awakens within, your being and consciousness open up in ways you couldn't imagine. The transformation allows the divine source of your true nature to break through your physical being into the world and into your conscious awareness. It is this

direct experience and contact with divinity that is the subject of nearly all the mystics and sages of the various religions and traditions.
Considering this as our context for what is mystical, there have been
numerous such happenings and experiences on my path. Lastly, the
word most appropriately shares a linguistic and contextual root with
the word mystery. I can't think of a better word to associate with this
tale. After all, one thing we know for sure about spirituality and the
mysteries of life, is how much we don't know. So, here you have it. To
the best of my ability, I document and present my mystical, spiritual
awakening story.

The Window

AS MENTIONED IN the Introduction, Part One of this book is going to largely focus on the roughly two-year period in which I began going through an energetic awakening. It involves a range of dramatic physical changes and the related mystical experiences associated with them. I will provide a brief sketch of my prior years, which is most of my life, to give this story a little more context, particularly as it relates to the general theme of spirituality and awakening.

Growing up, I was loosely raised Catholic. Religion was a secondary theme in my family, and for the most part, church attendance was sporadic at best. I did go to the confirmation classes and get "confirmed" at age thirteen, but that was the peak of my early involvement with religion. In all honesty, none of it had any real meaning to me at all. Church felt more like a chore, than anything. My heart was never invested in it, and therefore never meaningfully moved by it. When it became my choice whether to pursue religion or not, it quickly fell away.

I did, however, discover a most profound truth at that same age. After going through some pretty heavy emotional events that a child of divorce might face, I had a life changing insight. "It's all about love," I realized, "the whole secret to life is love." I still clearly remember sitting in my basement alone, saying that aloud to myself. Of course, this was a conceptual or intellectual understanding, and not a practice I was successfully integrating in my life. Like most of us, I would make a lovely mess of living it over the decades to come! It was a breakthrough nonetheless, as I knew it to be true, and it would stay with me always. Love is always the answer to anything that life presents, and the key is to figure out how in each instant. This basic life philosophy surely influenced my attraction to the hippie flower power culture, and my choice to live in places like Madison, WI and Berkeley, CA. As an English major in college, I read and studied a great deal of old literature. This included language study, scriptures, myths, epics, and philosophy. I really enjoyed it, but it was still largely academic.

The spark of my own genuine interest into all things spiritual would really begin in my mid-twenties. This would be a fulcrum point on my overall spiritual awakening path, and would be instigated by the study of Sacred Geometry. A coworker friend of mine shared some of his materials on the subject and I was quickly hooked. I studied it in depth for several years, and it turned out to be the right teaching for me at the right time. Due to its mathematical nature, it was a spiritual teaching that allowed me to enter the subject from a left-brain, logic-based perspective. My heart knew that there was a unity, to which love was the key, but my dominant mind was not sufficiently convinced. Sacred Geometry was a way to concretely demonstrate the oneness of all life to the logical mind, enough to inspire and facilitate an inquiry into unity and spirituality with a more holistic, complete approach. I dove in deeply, reading all my old texts and scriptures from multiple cultures and religions in a new light. I was particularly drawn to American Indian spirituality and its way of conveying divinity and expressing unity. I explored various divination systems for a span as well, like the I-Ching, Medicine cards, and Runes.

In 2004, at age twenty-six, I was living in Berkeley, CA working as a teacher and going through a divorce. My older friend, whom I'll call Berkeley Tom, was visiting me as I struggled with the dissolution of my marriage. He was very kind, had a warm smile, and baby pure, inviting eyes. He and his wife had taken multiple trips to India over the years, listening to and meditating with various sages. He would trigger my first notable mystical experience. He asked if he could touch my heart, to connect to and perhaps help release some of my emotional pain. With full trust, I gave him my permission. He placed his hand on my chest... within a few seconds, tears began to run down his face and then he was fully, audibly weeping. I felt a distinct heart-opening sensation in my chest and was weeping aloud with him in short order. All the pain and heartache surrounding my divorce came gushing out with ferocity. We stood there face to face, in this beautifully intimate connection, purging together. It was complete and cathartic. The despair and agony released would exit my open heart and never return. Some aspect of that encounter would result in a new found emotional peace and stability that would be with me from that day forward. Not surprisingly, it invigorated my spiritual journey and sparked a deeper investigation of Indian and Eastern religions and philosophy.

For the next phase in my spiritual development, I'll jump the story ahead to 2012. At this point, for context, I am a forty-four year old singer/songwriter who earns a livelihood as a freelance audio engineer, living in Topanga, CA. Of the places I have lived, it is where I have felt most at home and even the greatest sense of belonging, despite my strong hermit tendencies. I remain in the same studio apartment from when I initially moved here, which I have dubbed the "g-bubble." As I resume the narrative, I'll provide a general sense of my spiritual trajectory and orientation towards life. I was a genuinely happy man, with an inner peace that was mostly unaffected by the ups and downs of life. I had loved and lost several times, changed careers, and struggled to survive as many of us do. Over many years, in living into my initial realization that "it was all about love," I had landed in a beautiful heart space. I felt blessed to be alive and an intimate connection with humanity, Spirit, and the natural world. Graciously, I would often be appreciated for my calm and peaceful presence, and was regularly consulted by those in my life struggling with various issues.

By now I sensed more distinctly that I sometimes had a healing effect on people and circumstances, and even suspected that I had "healing hands." In the summer of 2012, I would put those hands to the test. A friend of mine was struggling to process a challenging, long-standing emotional trauma. With her permission, I sat beside her and began to connect to the disharmonious energy, as if I knew what I was doing. In actuality I did not, and just flowed spontaneously in action by instinct. Holding my hands above her, with my eyes closed, I clearly perceived a dark, murky energy field emerge as she wordlessly put her attention on the trauma. Breathing deeply and rhythmically, I had one hand connected to the energy and the other to the Earth. For several minutes, I inhaled the energy out of her field and exhaled it into the Earth. To both of our delights, the healing session was dramatically effective. She physically sensed the absence of the energy blockage that she had carried with her for so long. Her being was globally lightened, and some long absent measure of peace returned to her heart. It was visibly apparent to me as well. Whatever was healed would never return.

Over the next several years, I would continue to be sporadically asked for healing help, and life seemed to be getting progressively more mystical. Most notably, I discovered the profound truth that physical distance or separation was irrelevant with regard to healing. I was able to affect physical healing relief over long distance by connecting to a person's energy field. Several times I was able to help ameliorate headaches or stomach pain from afar. In a more dramatic example, I did a remote healing that involved sharing in the sensation of the symptom. A friend having a severe bout of vertigo lay at home seeking some relief. I lay on my couch, tuned into my own energy field, and then connected to her unstable field. In so doing, I was able to experience the dramatic physical symptom of imbalance for myself. Her overall "field" had a perceptible wobble from various energetic facets moving disharmoniously relative to each other. The energetic body has a plethora of fields and movements, which is the subject of another book entirely. I breathed "life force" into our connected fields and until they reached a harmonious resonance. When I no longer felt the wobble, I stopped. I would later learn that the challenging bout would take a dramatic turn for the better. My friend would actually get up shortly and go for a run.

By 2016, the mystical component of my journey was becoming more prevalent in my daily life. One noticeable trend was the nature of my contact with animals. I have always had a close connection with the animal kingdom, dogs in particular, but things were getting a little out of the ordinary. I was seemingly becoming something of an animal magnet. I live by myself, and actually have no pets of my own, but had animals visiting my apartment daily. Typically, I keep my door ajar for fresh air, and neighborhood animals were constantly just walking in and hanging out for a while. This includes a vast array of dogs and cats, including ones I'd never met until they were on my couch. I even noticed coyotes hanging around my door in the middle of the night with greater regularity. Multiple species of birds living in the trees outside my door would land and hop about right next to me without a care. I have absolutely cherished this blessed, intimate animal communion. On two separate occasions a pair of unknown, large dogs showed up at my door having gotten lost from a neighboring ridge over a mile away. They came in, jumped on me, and then lied down like they were prepared to stay forever. Many times I had to call owners and have them come pick up their dogs, which were sometimes reluctant to leave. Animals are known to be highly sensitive to energy and, for whatever reason, found mine to be increasingly agreeable and approachable.

During this time period, there were also a growing number of human interactions that were out of the ordinary and trending toward the mystical. I started being engaged by strangers fairly regularly. On multiple occasions I was stopped by people on the street for spiritual help, rather than the normal request for financial aid. I was mistaken for Jesus a number of times, though I grant that I do have what can be considered Jesus hair! I patiently listened to a few confessions, was asked about deceased loved ones, and even to relay messages to the spirit world. On other occasions, I had strangers randomly commenting on the high vibratory nature of my energy field. People would strike up a conversation with me and quickly launch into a description of a medical issue, and sometimes even ask directly for a healing.

These encounters became more frequent and would occur wherever I happened to be... in town, at the beach, or on a random errand. There was even someone who showed up at my door once, without knowing why or how they came to be standing there themselves. Yes, I know... any of the above-mentioned incidents can be reasonably explained away as an isolated incident. It is no surprise that animals like nice people! There may have been mental illness or substance abuse causing others to approach me in these ways. Some people simply open up and tell you more intimate things if you have an inviting personality or presence. Yes, this is all quite true and reasonable. However, the frequency of these occurrences, coupled with my prior healing experiences, told me that there was something deeper at play. My life was clearly unfolding on some mystical path, with its increasing profound encounters and insights, and yet it all remained largely enshrouded in mystery.

One of my primary audio gigs at this time was doing live sound engineering for a fairly large church community. It involved setting up, operating, and tearing down a substantial sound system for a full band in a large auditorium in Santa Monica. As soon as the gear was packed up and stored, I raced to an old cathedral in downtown L.A. for an evening service. It is a beautiful space. Again it required a full sound system setup, but first I had to make room for a full band by clearing the altar space in the cathedral. It was a very tight time window between the two locations, and I was always in a hurry. So, it would be extra tight on Easter Sunday of 2017, with the additional pressure of the import of the day. My setup was the largest of the year and the cathedral had the most stuff to clear. When I got to the cathedral that afternoon, it had already been vacated and locked up. I was the first of my crew to arrive and had keys, so I entered, flipped on the lights, and got to work. There were flower boxes, stands, statues, ornate candles, and crosses. I grabbed an item in each hand and made numerous rapid clearing trips. Finally, only two items remained. I grabbed the hundred and fifty year-old gold cross with my left hand, and reached for a painted wooden flower stand box with my right.

Swooping my arm down, I reached into the hollow underside of the box so I could pick it up with my one free hand, and... ouch!

A rusty old nail on the inside of the box went right through the center of my palm, with great force. Technically, it didn't go all the way through. It reached the other side of my hand, but did not break the skin. I instinctively yanked my hand back and dropped the box. It hurt a lot and it was a gusher! Blood was dripping all over the well-maintained wood floor. I clenched my fist to try and stop the flow, and then froze on my feet in awe of the moment. There I stood alone in the solemn silence of this beautiful old cathedral... in the altar space that occupies the center of the crucifix-shaped building, holding a gold cross in one hand, and bleeding from a nail hole in the palm of the other. For good measure, I looked up to confirm that I was standing under a massive suspended image of Jesus on the cross... and it's Easter Sunday. I mean, stuff happens, but come on! A stigmata-referencing wound on Easter? If you've ever had one of those happenings in your life when you think that it somehow had to be scripted, you'll have an idea of what I was feeling. Even if we are clueless as to the mysterious writer, most people sense or acknowledge some other intelligence or consciousness at work in our lives other than our own. I use the phrase stigmata-referencing purposefully, so as not to confuse what will be a common theme in this story with how we traditionally understand the stigmata. Traditionally, holy Saints who have received stigmata, so fully identified with the suffering of Christ and meaning of the Cross, bring into manifestation all five of the wounds in their full measure... or full glory. In my story, the "references" are like signposts for the wayfarer, validations and confirmations along the incomprehensible and mysterious journey.

One character merits an introduction before I launch into the energetic awakening portion of my story. It was actually just shortly after Easter when a neighborhood cat, that I had seen from afar a few times, decided to make friends. She is beautiful... a black cat with vibrant green eyes and a heavenly purr. She is here right now as I type! We got to know each other slowly. She was not one for much affection at first, but after a while her visits lengthened and she started lingering and taking naps. I learned that she lived in the house down the street that was always bustling with the energy of excitable young kids and three constantly barking dogs. I think she was coming by to get away from all the drama and enjoy some peace and quiet! This was my first relationship of note with a cat, and as is the case with all of God's creatures, there is much to learn from observing a cat! In any event, she would soon learn that I was an easy mark, as before long I found myself buying dry cat food and supplementing her breakfast. I named her Shakti Kitty, after the divine Goddess, who can be considered the personification of both the energy of creation and the creation itself. This name will make more sense as you read of her ongoing role in the rest of this unfolding story.

In the closing months of 2017, though I did not know it at the time, an energetic awakening and physical transformation had begun in earnest. I knew next to nothing about such things as energetic awakenings, light body activations, or the arising of kundalini energy. To me, the medical adventure that I am about to relay was simply that. In the fall, I noticed a few new and interesting medical issues. I dealt with them and paid them no mind. After all, I was approaching my fiftieth birthday, and things were bound to arise in the physical body. First, my eyesight improved dramatically. I had been wearing progressively stronger eyewear for thirty-five years, and suddenly my glasses were way too strong. The eye doctor said I was simply experiencing "second sight," and we reduced the strength of my prescription. On the other hand, my hearing got worse. In my right ear only, I had some profound hearing loss in the upper frequency range. I was thoroughly examined, including a head MRI, and nothing relevant was discovered. There was a constant white noise present, which would ebb and flow in intensity. When I sit quietly and tune into it, it oddly sounds like chirping crickets in the distance. Moreover, it not only impacted volume, but also pitch or frequency. When I move a tuning fork from my normal ear to my effected ear, the pitch of the sound noticeably rises in vibration. Lastly, I began to experience bouts of lightheadedness. Certain head motions would consistently produce a several second dizzy spell. This phenomenon would come and go in waves for several years.

In general, I have been blessed with very good health for as long as I can remember. I almost never caught a cold, let alone got really sick. When I did, I would bounce back in a couple of days. I took no medications and probably only a handful of aspirin over my entire adulthood. In January of 2018, I contracted a cold during flu season that wouldn't go away. I was physically drained yet struggling to sleep, and I largely lost my appetite. Somehow I seemed to be putting on an unusual amount of weight, but I attributed it to being sedentary for several weeks. I also began having increased roving muscular pain in my upper body that would become intense enough to where I couldn't lie down. I decided to go to the doctor to make sure that I didn't have pneumonia or something else. It was my first doctor visit in nearly thirty years! I was examined and told it was just a tough flu strain, but they would do a chest x-ray to be certain. Nothing was found, but by grace or good fortune, the doctor thought the shadow of my heart looked a little large and referred me to cardiology. I went to the hospital and had all the relevant tests, scans, and lab work.

My problem was pericardial effusion... the sac that contains the heart was severely enlarged from inflammation and fluid retention. My actual heart was fine, but was getting increasingly compressed. All my glands were going wild, especially in my torso, and I had gained a good fifteen pounds of fluid throughout my body. I had obvious edema (swelling) in my legs, ankles, and feet. I was told they had three standard drug protocols to deal with the effusion symptom, and we would start the first one immediately. It works about 95% of the time, the doctor noted, and in the worst-case scenario they would simply drain it with a needle to relieve the pressure. Having never taken much more than a few aspirin in my life, I was about to learn the power of pharmaceutical drugs. Meanwhile, the entire cardiology team was gathering to figure out what was causing my condition. So far, all of the tests showed nothing... it was some kind of inflammatory virus, they said.

For several months, I gutted out all three of the drug protocols. We started with obscene amounts of ibuprofen... nothing. Then we tried something stronger... nothing. Finally, I endured a powerful steroid... nothing. Taking these drugs was as brutal as the condition itself. With every dose, I felt like I was knowingly ingesting poison. I was a complete mess. I was itching from head to toe from the constantly changing tension in my skin, I was in pain from the pressure in my chest, I couldn't sleep, and I was tweaked from the hardcore meds. My body energy was volatile, and I continued to swell. During this time there were repeated trips to the hospital to monitor inflammation, take labs, and do diagnostic scans. By now the staff of the infectious disease department was on the case, checking for various viruses both common and rare... still nothing. The drugs hadn't worked, I was still producing a lot of fluid, and now it was time to drain it with a needle to relieve the mounting pressure on the heart. As it happened, I wasn't a candidate for the simpler procedure. During all of the scans, it was discovered that long before the current effusion, my heart sac had been carrying more fluid than optimal. Over many years, the space had "organized," growing into separate areas and creating multiple pockets of fluid. It would require multiple draining sites. They planned to do it the following week, but I couldn't wait that long.

I was out of my mind with angst and agony, and was admitted into the hospital through the ER on the day before Easter of 2018. I went to a different hospital in my network to be closer to my sister, who was likely the reason I was still alive at this point. That means another staff of cardiologists and infectious disease doctors got a crack at my case. Ultimately, they wouldn't be able to diagnose me either, but they sure tried. They grew cultures, checked foreign illnesses, and I was seemingly tested for everything. But, going back to my acute condition upon arrival, they would have to give draining the sac a shot. Two different cardiologists with two different techniques took a turn. After being pierced multiple times over several failed efforts, we found a method that was effective enough to do several times. It was quite painful and felt utterly medieval! They pierced the chest, without any anesthetic, and managed to jam a tube into one of the pocket areas. I rolled around in a full circle in both directions, in an attempt to get fluid to seep into the area with the drain. All the while, a painful suction force was being applied to draw out what they could. My eyes rolled back in my head more than once during this barbaric scene, but when they refocused I had the blessing to behold my loving family, who had flown in from around the country. The doctor and I worked hard and drained vast amounts of the bloody fluid. So much so, that we filled all of the beakers in the room and we had to pause to restock. Of course, here I am on Easter weekend, being pierced in the left side to drain fluid and blood. The mysterious synchronicity did not escape my perception. Outrageously, it appears that my bizarre, Holy Week stigmata streak continued...

Despite our success and efforts, I was still producing large amounts of fluid due to my undiagnosed virus. Life saving surgery was necessary in a matter of days. Thankfully, it was to be of the thoracic rather than open-heart variety. The surgeon would drain as much fluid as he could, scrape and remove as much pocket creating growth as possible, and cut a permanent window in the sac so fluid couldn't accumulate and aversely affect the heart. Instead, it would drain into the pulmonary and abdominal areas and would be more easily handled by the body. I lay in the noisy ICU, itching and entirely uncomfortable, awaiting surgery. My family was valiantly taking shifts so I was never alone, even through the night. I should add right here that the intimate family time was absolutely wonderful and produced as many tears of beauty as were produced by agony. In fact, throughout the entire ordeal, my inner peace and joy was unwavering. I was fully surrendered to the circumstances and the will of Spirit, learning valuable lessons about life and myself, relishing my close relationships, and extracting beauty from adversity. I considered it an advanced course in the School of Life, and I was determined to make the most of it... though I was hoping it was only a one-semester class!

On the night before my surgery, things would get a little mystical. I was enduring another sleepless night with my sister, gabbing and passing the time, resting when possible. I was somewhat bonkers from lack of sleep and the perilous state of my body, but still relatively alert. I was lying still in the bed, breathing rhythmically, trying to keep it together. My sister, bless her gracious heart, was lying on the ICU floor. She had folded a blanket into quarters, and was curled up on it like a dog bed. At some point I began feeling like my consciousness was only tenuously attached to my physical body. It didn't leave the body or observe the scene from the outside, but was largely detached from the physical form. It was like I was witnessing myself from within myself. My body was highly energized, and that energy was the only sensation that held my attention. It was a lovely, ethereal feeling and it filled the entire space of the room. I don't know how I was presenting on the outside, but I was smiling with awe and wonder on the inside. Then I perceived a brilliant, shimmering, green energy slowly begin to fill the room from the top down. It was filling like an upside-down swimming pool. My eyes were open, and as far as I was concerned, I was seeing the field in the actual room. I was enthralled and impatiently excited for the energy to reach my body. I stretched my arms up in the air as high as I could, so I could touch the energy field as soon as possible. It would fill the entire space, and my body was joyously engulfed.

My sister, who witnessed this event, would later add her perspective. She reported that this scene lasted for nearly fifteen minutes, with a constant stream of audible mumbling and multiple occurrences of skyward arm reaching. She thought I was delirious, coming in and out of consciousness, but every few minutes we would lock eyes in recognition of each other. She was rather terrified, as the only word she could clearly discern in my rambling was "light," and I kept reaching out longingly. She was struck by the obvious possibility that I may have been dropping the body for good. I do recall my sister standing right by my bedside when I was more stably back in my body and the energy had dissipated. Her warm smile was the first thing I would see. To my astonishment, I was sure that I had awoken into a different room. Everything looked different… my view, the door, the window, the space outside the room, etc… The only constant was the presence of my sister, whom I immediately addressed. "This isn't the same room," I insisted, "What happened? When did we move? Did I miss something?" She listened attentively with a degree of fascination at my claim, but calmly reassured me that she thought it was the same room, and that we had in fact, not moved. I found her credible. However, looking through my eyeballs, it definitely looked like a different room!

I had surgery on April 6th, 2018. It went very well. The surgeon was amazing and impressively executed the procedure like a highly sophisticated video game. He made four entry holes in my chest… one for a camera, one for a drain, and two for his tools. As planned, a lot of fluid was drained and much obstructive growth was scraped and removed. Most critically, a window was cut in the heart sac to prevent it from simply filling back up, as the cause of my increased fluid production remained undiagnosed. The window was the key to giving my body a chance to handle the vast physical changes and adjust to the new flows of energy. Bravo, doctor! You have my gratitude. The relief from the operation was dramatic and most welcomed. There was much less pressure in my chest and my heart was no longer being dangerously compressed. For the next week or so, they would monitor how the rest of my body was handling the fluid that had been redirected from the window surgery. I regained enough strength to walk around a bit, and was mercifully released to recover at home. I was still laden with a large amount of fluid throughout my body, but as my unhindered heart strengthened, it would be able to act more effectively on the fluid. That was the hope, as they still didn't know what was wrong with me. I still had no idea, myself. At this point I considered my greatest hurdle the insistence that I take a brutal medication that I had grown to despise, for three more long months. They said it was necessary to prevent my now deflated heart sac from sticking to the organ like a popped bubble, forcing them to crack my chest and peel it off. I agreed to take the poison.

The next two months trying to recover at home was a struggle.

The operation had removed the life-threatening danger, but I was in bad shape, still very weak, with significant inflammation throughout my body. The window was serving its purpose, and my body was holding its own. I could tell that while I wasn't getting any worse, I wasn't really getting any better, either. I was dutifully taking the powerful medication, despite knowing that it was wreaking havoc on my body. How could I recover from my illness if my body needs all of its energy to deal with the poison I kept ingesting? Moreover, due to the itching and manic effects of the drug, I could barely sleep. So, I was also missing out on this most critical healing time when the sleeping body is at rest. I gutted it out for two months and then stopped taking everything… I would take matters into my own hands. I had been further taxing the body when it most needed its power and strength. The body's natural intelligence knew exactly what to do, and just needed the energy to do it. I had plenty of time on my hands during those recuperative months, and tried to gain a better understanding of what was happening to me. Perhaps the medical community couldn't find an answer because the physical symptoms didn't have a physical cause. There had been a clear mystical thread running through the adventure, so maybe this was something spiritual in nature rather than merely physical.

Despite all of the drama and difficulty presented by my condition, from a spiritual perspective I considered myself profoundly blessed and inherently happy. I knew the joy and beauty of acting from the heart rather than the mind, with love always as the tip of the spear. I felt a deep love and connection to life, and was aware of the divine nature and greater potential of being human. Although I had been interested in and studying various spiritual texts and teachings for decades, I knew almost nothing of an energetic awakening. I was familiar with some of the paradigms used to describe this phenomenon, such as kundalini awakening, ascension, or the immaculate birth of the Christ or Shakti within, but had no real concept of it as a lived experience. I took a deeper dive into these teachings and the writings of the mystics of various religions and traditions. It was clear to me that they were using different words and models to point to the same thing... a singular core truth about the divine nature of a human being and the potentialities of its expression in the physical world or phenomenal plane. My entire medical adventure, with its physical and energetic changes and symptoms, began to make sense. I was seeing it in a new light, part of a greater spiritual process that was unfolding.

I would no longer sit around waiting to heal, but would place all of my energy on healing myself, or more accurately, creating a space in which the body could heal itself. First, I had stopped all medications. Second, I committed to taking a walk on the beach every day, regardless of how short. I was extremely weak in the beginning, and it was all I could do to make it from my car to the sand. There was no walking initially, but just breathing the ocean air and taking in the sublime beauty was wonderful and healing. There's something divinely magical about the way the four basic elements of earth, air, fire, and water come together at the coast. This quickly became the most cherished part of my day. As my strength increased and my fluid decreased, my beach walks lengthened. It became my healing medicine walk... a walking meditation with my bare feet in the sand, relishing the sacred connection to Mother Earth. Another key component to the healing process was becoming more conscious of my diet. Most of my life I have pretty much just eaten whatever I wanted, in sporadic but large portions, with little concern for content. After being hospitalized and barely eating from long spans of appetite loss, I had a dietary reset. My body had become very sensitive to all inputs. It was true for medications and equally true for food, and I was noticing how everything I put in my mouth was affecting my body. It was a new dynamic for me, and old cravings vanished as new ones arose. I was relearning my body, and increasingly eating what it was asking for, as opposed to what I wanted to taste. I have placed no dietary restrictions on myself, but pay attention and listen to my body like never before. Nowadays, I find myself eating mostly fruit.

A final, most critical, aspect of my healing efforts was the focused attention on communicating with my body. When I wasn't walking on the beach, I was engaged in trying to vitalize and strengthen my energy field, so the body could do its work. I did a lot of rhythmic breathing and sitting in silence, consciously drawing in or channeling life force to my field. I directly engaged my physical body and all of its intricate strata of life and consciousness. I talked to my organs, my blood, my glands, and even my individual cells. There was a continuous open dialogue happening in which I was feeding them source energy, love, and gratitude. We weren't trying to solve anything or figure it all out, but rather just healing like it was a foregone conclusion and enjoying the miraculous nature of it all. And it was remarkable. After a month of my new healing protocol, I was feeling dramatically better! My strength was up, the fluid was down, and I felt a new vitality in my energy field. I was also aware that whatever was happening to me was just beginning. In my dialogue with my total being, I made it clear that we weren't stopping at better… we were going to blow past the old normal and heal fully on this magical transformational journey.

For the rest of 2018, and really from then on, a new pattern would emerge as a new type of healing was underway. I felt amazing, and was surging with energy like never before… so much so that I wasn't sleeping very much, yet it didn't matter as it was to no physical detriment. It was as if a powerful light switch had been turned on inside my body that would never be turned off. Voluminous amounts of high vibratory light and energy were being recognized by and incorporated into my physical form. It was clear that everything I had been through was preparing my body to handle or channel more "life force." Had it not been for the preexisting condition of my compromised heart sac, I may have weathered the changes without the medical drama, but perhaps not. Of course I know everything that happens is no mistake, but rather part of a mysterious, divine orchestration. Thankfully, the window surgery had saved my life.

I soon discovered that the permanent, high voltage energy that was turned on in my body was on a dimmer switch, and this was the low setting. As soon as I would stabilize the newly heightened energy, the dimmer switch would get turned up. There would be a surge of energy to the current limits of the body, accompanied by various physical symptoms and angst. Once a certain level of stabilization was reached, the juice would get turned up further and the process repeat. I'm not going to get bogged down in describing all the physical symptoms and movements associated with an energetic awakening... that is its own book, and many such books have already been written. I will say a few words about the well-documented phenomena of "kriyas," or involuntary movements or expressions of the body relative to energetic awakenings. When the energy moves through the body, it is opening or reactivating new and latent channels. As it does it's "rewiring" work, it runs into energy blockages that are being held in the body. All sorts of spontaneous actions may occur as the energy seeks to break through or dissolve the obstructions. The causes of such energy blocks are numerous, and may be physical, emotional, or mental. This is another vast subject, and volumes have already been written about it. The kriyas I experienced were mostly physical, and included muscle spasms, cramps, jolts of shooting energy, and the body moving into very specific positions. I would soon discover that surrender was the key. In my experience, letting go and flowing with the movements was the most effective way of handling these phenomena as they did their necessary work.

The Slideshow

DURING THE ONGOING phases of the transformation, awakening, and healing, though it was often quite challenging, I had a renewed sense of joy and wonderment. I didn't know in the traditional scientific way what was happening to me, yet at the same time I knew on some deeper level. Something absolutely amazing was unfolding... something sacred was revealing itself, and I definitely did not want to get in the way. I took a posture of full surrender to the process and the energy itself, from a place of love and gratitude for this magnificent blessing. One day while I was strolling the beach with my head in the proverbial clouds, the mystical component of the journey would again take center stage, giving rise to this story within a story. I was growing accustomed to being approached by strangers, but the following encounter was most memorable and profound.

It was an absolutely gorgeous southern California day. The sun shone brightly in the clear blue sky over the glistening sea. I had just taken a refreshing dip in the ocean and was standing at the waters edge. I turned my gaze inland to where the boulders lead up to Pacific Coast Highway, and espied an older gentleman who began climbing down the rocks from where he had been sitting. He made his way down to the sand and walked across the beach directly towards me as I watched. He arrived with a warm smile, introduced himself, and told me the following: He lived in the valley and hadn't been to the beach in many years. He felt strangely compelled to come on this day, so he decided to sit on the rocks and look at the ocean. He said he was a happy man and in very good spirits, despite recently receiving some troubling news from his doctor. He continued that when he saw me exit the water, he saw a turquoise ball of light vaguely concealing a man rather than a person. He knew this must sound crazy, but he also knew in his heart that he had come to the beach to see me. He was completely blown away by what was happening, but here he was.

Little did he know that I was equally blown away, having seen his appearance, gait, mannerisms, and hearing him speak! A dear friend of mine, Dino, had passed away the year before. This guy, in all the ways just listed, was a spitting image of my friend. To portray Dino would require multiple chapters and still fail miserably. I'll just say I miss him and love that our lives intersected. Hurricane Dino... the quintessential bull in a china shop... my old school, overly affectionate friend, with his dominant east coast Italian personality and a frantic, disheveled presence. He was the kind of man who would lay down his life for family, and he considered everyone to be family. He was a wonderful friend, but also a rather tortured soul. He battled cancer like a champ for years before dropping the body. This guy on the beach had it all... the same clothing style and body shape, the same pronounced knee limp, the same distinct facial hair pattern and grayness, the same way of talking with his hands, and clearly, the same fearless personal engagement skills. "Hello brother," I said smiling warmly, "We both got here right on time. I must be here to see you too." His eyes were tearing up, but he was totally giddy, and he bear-hugged me on the spot and kissed me on the cheek... very Dino!

He would spend the next several minutes enthusiastically expressing his newfound peace and happiness. He had clearly just had some insight or realization about the unity of life, and was experiencing a profound sense of oneness. He was essentially trying to convey the idea of Heaven on Earth and could hardly contain himself. I knew this place well, as I have seen it blossom in others and felt it myself. Periodically he would pause and seem to be looking for some kind of confirmation from me. I would oblige, as I was hearing what I considered to be some wonderful truths being spoken. The stranger would embrace me again and tell me he loved me. Of course, I responded to my brother in kind, still fascinated by his uncanny resemblance to my dearly departed friend. It was like I was talking to Dino… without the baggage of the life story, without the soul torment, and with the peace that my old friend so frantically pursued. I felt his presence, as if he were trying to show me that he was ok now.

The man leaned in closer. He said that he was fine and happy to die at any time, but he had just gotten some tough medical news from his doctor. There was something in his neck near the top of his spine that, if hit or triggered the wrong way, could kill him instantly. "I'm ok," he said, "but I think that is what I was supposed to tell you." "Show me," I replied. He turned and tilted his head, exposing the back of his neck, awaiting my action. Instinctively, I placed my left hand on his heart, and my right hand on the back of his neck. We stood there silently, eyes locked, and the intensity of the energy in that space increased with every breath. His eyes were like those of a newborn… innocent, pure, and empty, yet with a deep and vast fullness. I was intending healing love and light into his heart and neck when I felt a great surge of energy hit my body. A translucent shaft of green light descended through the top of my head from above, passed through my heart center, and then flowed through my hands into my brother standing before me. I could perceive the shaft of green energy as clearly as I felt the air in my lungs and the earth under my feet. There was a beautiful healing going on, and I was utterly filled with joy. It was also clear that I wasn't doing the healing, but rather something divinely orchestrated was operating on both the man and me at the same time. We stayed like this for several minutes. I lowered my arms, but held my gaze on my brother, now weeping. "No one has ever looked at me that way in my life… so deeply," he said. "It's like you were looking at my soul. What did you see," he asked? "I saw myself, brother," I replied with a warm smile. He delighted in the response. Thanking me profusely, he gave me hug, grabbed my head in his hands, kissed my forehead, and proceeded to skip joyously up the coast… awkward limp and all. It didn't seem as if he were even touching the ground. I don't know what he actually experienced or learned from his encounter with the turquoise man, but I certainly had a lesson-filled, healing experience of my own.

For me, this event was something of a fulcrum point in my spiritual awakening story. I simultaneously felt the sensation of completion or closure, and one of absolute newness or opening... one circle of life giving way to another. What was closing? The medical adventure that threatened my very life, many old paradigms and behaviors, and my perception of my role in the world, to name a few... all resolved in that powerful encounter. What was new and opening? Everything. Absolutely everything... the further blossoming of my already joyful heart, my growing understanding of the potential of the human being, an awareness of consciousness previously unperceived, and the unfolding of a new sense of purpose that remained a magical mystery. I could sense that all I had experienced to date, including the transformational physical and energetic changes, was necessary to allow the mystical beach experience to happen. As the energetic or light body activates, it can provide a channel or portal through which higher vibratory energies can operate. There is no human healer really, but a space can manifest or open in a human being, such that there is an opportunity for a healing to occur. Spirit, or source energy, will take or leave that opportunity, based on its supreme intelligence and divine will... or, as I tend to call it, Grace. And so 2018, which started with limitation and darkness, would end with a newfound liberation in a glorious blaze of light. It was a beautiful year of growth on the path of discovery and awakening. Of course, it was but another wave of my unfolding journey. A new year was fast approaching, and the mystic dimmer switch was about to get cranked!

Everything that had happened to me thus far to expand my conscious awareness and raise the vibratory rate of my energetic body, was so the next series of events could occur. At the beginning of 2019, I had what I will call three heart activations in a six-week span. If we are to define a mystic encounter as a lived experience of the divine within, this was it. This is a game changer on the awakening path in which the divine vibration of source energy, which is pure love, awakens in your heart and explodes with bliss in every cell of your body. This experience has and can be described using a variety of spiritual models… the rapture of the Holy Spirit, the chakra opening activity of the active Kundalini, the divine marriage of Shiva and Shakti, the Immaculate Conception, union with Christ, discovery of your true Buddha nature, and on and on and on. They all work for me, as they are essentially pointing to the same thing, but they also carry a lot of excess cultural baggage that often veils their simple truth. We humans love and value complexity so much, that we often struggle to discern that which is exceedingly simple. I will endeavor to describe what these activation events were like, but the inadequacy of words has never felt so glaringly obvious.

The first instance happened in late January. At this time, I was feeling globally wonderful. It was just one year after the activation of my energetic body had caused my physical body to start transforming, sending me to the hospital. I felt healthier than ever in my life and was stably integrating the higher vibratory energy levels. I lay down on my couch to begin the process of getting some sleep. I say process, because it was taking me two to three hours to fall asleep due to the high current of energy that flowed unceasingly through my body since this whole thing began. When I first lay down, and my body and mind find their repose, the high energy current remains and is therefore more pronounced. I typically surrender to it… offer myself to Spirit so it can do it's work of "rewiring" the body while it is at rest. There were sometimes kriyas arising and frequent jolts or pulses of current in my legs. No matter how tired I was when I laid down, soon I would be vibrantly wide-awake. After several hours I would fall asleep for a four-hour block if I was lucky.

On this night, the energy had something else in mind. After just a few minutes of natural rhythmic breathing, I was pleasantly feeling atypically grounded and relaxed. I felt a deep gratitude in my heart for my life and all of its blessings. Then it happened. A vibration emerged in my heart of immense, unspeakable bliss. It quickly welled up in intensity and exploded out of every cell in my body. It was the vibration of love, so incredibly pure and powerful that I knew that I was being introduced to divinity itself. My entire body was resonating with this magnificent source energy and I was overcome with an ecstatic bliss that is beyond description. It felt like God had opened a door to infinity in my spiritual heart, and all of the love in the universe flooded in. I lay in the "blissfield," which was both inside and outside of my body, and all space paradoxically collapsed into it and arose from it simultaneously. Tears of joy and bliss erupted from my being with a force I had never before experienced. I began audibly wailing beyond my control. I was practically yelling, my chest heaving, and I was powerless to do a thing about it. I lay vibrating in bliss, weeping in ecstasy for a good twenty minutes. All sense of separation was slipping away... I was in the blissfield, but I was also the very blissfield in which I lay. Whatever I had considered or conceived to be the perfect love in my wildest imagination was summarily laid to waste. Just a sliver of this powerful vibration was a million times greater and more profound.

My entire being filled with a deep gratitude, which presented physically as a distinct vibratory signature and bodily sensation, all within this substratum of source love energy. My heart overflowed with the joy of receiving in its purest form, and I felt immeasurably blessed to be gifted by Spirit in this way. I use the word Spirit here because it implies a formless presence or intelligence other than the one that I had previously considered to be mine. I was aware of myself laying there having an experience, and also of a divine energy acting upon the body from within. Then, as if I were being presented a slideshow, a vast series of people, events, and relationships flowed through my mind's eye. With each image or scene flashed, I could timelessly see the entire story of how that image moved my awakening path forward to where I could be laying there today in the divine blissfield. This form of cosmic communication, in which I am "downloaded" massive information or comprehensive knowledge in a flash, would become a regular occurrence on the awakening journey.

Immense gratitude flowed through me, tears still gushing from my eyes, and I thanked everyone for everything with all the power of my heart. It included people and events that one might expect to arise, but also some forgotten, more random happenings that one would never suspect. With every slide, Spirit was revealing all of the hows and whys, and I continued to express my deep gratitude. An inner, divine presence and intelligence had awoken in my heart, and opened a mystical doorway to the greater potentials of human consciousness. The feeling of ultimate bliss and love was the only thing in existence, and a sense of unity with all life pervaded my being. Somehow, I lay in this dimensionless blissfield, yet it lay in my dimensionless heart. I was moved by the will and grace of divine Spirit, yet I was that very Spirit, too. My heart lay open like the full spread of a blossomed flower... its petals opening on the surface of the ocean of bliss, and proceeding to float away from center. With this image in my mind's eye, I knew that it would never close again... It was impossible. The petals were gone, leaving a fully free and open heart to radiate its perfume and love, supplied by its infinite divine source.

This went on unceasingly... tears and bliss, love and gratitude, for a solid hour. I had been verbalizing my gratitude aloud, through the sobbing, as the lifetime of beautiful gifts I had received passed before me. Then, after a brief pause, I started to speak aloud again, but it was remarkably not the same "I" speaking. Unpacking and defining this "I" is better left for another time, whether you call it higher self, soul consciousness, Holy Spirit, or whatever. My experience in the moment was both simple and clear... a different intelligence than the one that's in standard operation was present, and action was flowing from its Will. It is beyond our thinking mind, and entirely incomprehensible to it. Out of my mouth came a series of teachings, insights, and lessons on a variety of issues related to the larger theme of gratitude. It was like one "aha" moment after another. This seemed to me an obvious channeling event, just like my experiences when receiving or transmitting energy during a healing, but it was being expressed verbally and concretely. It flowed from an innermost portal within the heart, rather than from the thinking mind. Words were not being formulated or thought out, but being supplied in the instant upon my lips. My mind was hearing them for the first time as they were spoken. It was surreal to say the least.

My awareness was dancing around the space, as the form, the witness, and the speaker. I was all of the diversity at once, and also the very space in which it arose. Everything was the blissful vibration of love in its full glory. The quality of the awakening was not one of transcending from one consciousness level to another, but rather an inclusive opening of consciousness to its more transcendent aspects. This episode lasted about an hour and a half. My body vibrated with a most intense current the entire time, and I wept profusely nonstop. I literally don't think my body could have handled much more, but Spirit in her wisdom knew just how far she could push it. This was a truly amazing breakthrough moment on the awakening path. I label this event "heart activation" because it sensationally arose from that bodily center and was evidence of a latent or potential function coming online, not because it meets some predefined definition. My energetic awakening and transformation had reached a vibration high enough to allow this potentiality to unfold. By her Grace, the divine Spirit that is the very vibration of love itself, made herself known. I used the word Spirit here, but will refer to or personify this cosmic intelligent presence in a number of ways throughout this story. Holy Spirit, Divine Mother, Shakti, and God are among a list of appropriate signifiers for this awakened consciousness. I believe this profound activation was a taste of what is meant by the flesh made divine, or Heaven on Earth... blissfully delicious. An entirely new strata of consciousness had awoken within and I would never be the same... a phrase that is sure to be repeated in these pages.

Several weeks later it would happen again. I had a full force heart activation event, exploding with love and accompanied by its sweet perfume of unspeakable bliss. This second activation would unfold in its own unique way and express its own particular signature or flavor of divine love. I was having a quiet morning at home, when I was graced by the presence of Shakti Kitty, who strolled in for some love and a snack. She visited almost daily and had clearly taken a deep interest in me. Kitty had been present throughout my energetic awakening process, including the entire medical adventure and healing from the outset. I was already convinced that she somehow knew what was going on with me. I think she could perceive the vast energy at play and wanted to be around it or otherwise involved. She was seemingly monitoring my progress and would often guard my door and conduct sweeps of the interior. On many occasions I saw her clearly tracking what I intuited to be an invisible energy or entity across the room. I had no doubt that Shakti Kitty was actively protecting me and maintaining the space in which I was undergoing this profound transformation.

Shakti knew that if she lay on the floor and stretched out, I would lie next to her and pet her. It was failsafe, and that's what she did on this February day. However, instead of our normal brief love exchange of pets and purrs, she stayed and poured on the affection like never before. It was a most beautiful communion. I was lying on my side petting her, when she drove her head into my heart center and purred with a powerful, heavenly vibration. Bliss and joy welled up inside and the love I felt for Kitty streamed down my face. She backed out twice and drove her head into my heart until I rolled over on my back. As I did, I literally said aloud to her, "Oh, you want me to lay on my back! Ok!" Right away, she laid across my legs like she was pinning me down, another totally unprecedented move. She closed her eyes and acted like she was fully asleep, knowing full well that I would never move and disturb her precious slumber. She had me right where she wanted me.

I didn't have a chance to move anyway, because almost immediately my heart would explode with energy again. I was suddenly fully resonating with and vibrating in the same blissfield of love as in the first activation. I wept profusely, beyond my control, as the supreme radiance of love moved through the divine door of the spiritual heart. This time, however, rather than the vibratory signature and teaching of gratitude, the emphasis was on that of love and communion in relationship. Somehow I knew that beyond any doubt. I peered down at Kitty, who had just perfectly instigated and illustrated that very teaching in the present moment. Then the slideshow of images, people, and scenes began, just like the last time. Lying in the bliss-field, I felt my love for all of the people in my life to the fullest measure, and the vast beauty of the receiving of that same love in return.

The purity of Divine Love is irrevocable, immensely beautiful, and also a jarring wakeup call. For though I have always considered myself one who loves to a high degree, I knew in this instant that I had never truly loved anyone. This is a tough pill to swallow and shall be swallowed by all who venture to this point on the path. It will trigger some unavoidable, deep inner work to clear the remaining energetic blockages in the hidden corners of the subtle emotional body. This is an ongoing and necessary process during the continuous refinement of an awakening journey. It's not all rose petals and bliss... but these heart activations were absolutely beatific! Again, all action was the movement of that divine intelligence within... flashing imagery, teachings, full-bodily ecstasy, and healing simultaneously. Kitty lay peacefully asleep on my legs, seemingly oblivious, effortlessly holding me in position. This activation event was much shorter than the first, lasting about thirty to forty minutes. When the vibration settled and my consciousness steadied in my body, I opened my eyes. I immediately looked at Shakti Kitty, who opened her eyes, jumped off, and strolled out the open door like I wasn't even there!

After a two-week gap I would get hit hard again, with another activation of equal astounding, divine power. It was late morning, and I was standing upright playing a set of music on the guitar. I hadn't played much at all for a year and was dusting off a few songs, trying to get my performance chops back. To my delight, it felt wonderful. I rocked a full set, and as I commonly close with a Dylan song, I launched into Knockin' On Heaven's Door, which I hadn't played in years. Once I began, my mind quickly went to the fact that less than a year ago I had a brush with death and was "knockin'" for real. Then that majestic, divine presence erupted in my heart, causing my entire being to tingle with bliss. In that glorious instant, Spirit communicated that now Heaven was knockin' on my door, and I was knockin' on Heaven's door… right now… while living and fully conscious. The door was open, and I fell into eternity.

I barely got my guitar off my shoulder without smashing it as I collapsed to the ground. The wave of love literally floored me. I joyously stretched out. Again, every cell in my body was humming, purring, and vibrating with ecstatic bliss beyond words. Tears of great beauty and joy flowed like rivers from my eyes. I lay in complete awe and surrender. Again, I am simultaneously aware through multiple lenses or dimensions of consciousness. I am the one on the floor, the awakened energy within, the witness of it all, and the space within which it all occurs. This is some kind of unity consciousness that doesn't transcend anything, but rather includes everything. It is the vibration of the source energy of all that is and the vibration of love itself. They are the same. It is another way of saying that God is Love, and it can be experienced in the awakened human physiology.

This third heart activation would unfold like the others, but have its own theme, lessons, and vibratory signatures. From within the joyous blissfield, arose a feeling of suffering that I felt deeply in my open heart. I could feel the pain and agony of suffering, but never detached from its rich depth and beauty. Everything that arises in the blissfield… which is everything… is made of beauty. Seen through an expansive enough lens, it is only beauty that is revealed in the unfolding of events. The slideshow of images, people, and events commenced, supporting and guiding this divinely inspired teaching. Without getting detailed, I felt in my heart the particular sufferings of specific people and events, as if they were my own… it was deeply heartbreaking, raw, and emotional. Again, I am associating the various shades of emotions with specific vibratory signatures. The suffering then reached peak intensity, as much as I could possibly take. Spirit spoke to my heart, saying that this was a taste of the global suffering of mankind, and its immensity bore that out. It was a most unique and unforgettable sensation with its own resonance... its quality indescribable and its power suffocating.

Mercifully, that taste was brief. At its peak, it transmuted into a glorious counterpart... pure compassion. The global suffering gave way to global compassion... passion for all. It was amazingly profound and its own sublime energetic wave moved through the ocean of bliss. It was revealed as both a communal and individual expression during the remainder of the activation event. To be clear, though this third event dealt with some darker themed emotions, never was there an absence of the tear producing bliss that engulfed me. No matter what emotion or sensation I was being shown, I was always peacefully cradled in the loving embrace of the divine essence that had emerged within. It was all immeasurably beautiful and an absolute divine blessing. This episode also included some audible channeling of related teachings that were blowing my mind as they came out. They came in rapid succession and were quickly forgotten, each engulfed in the brilliant flame of Truth of the next one. I'm sure that they will resurface right on time, if needed. I opened my eyes, felt myself in my body, and opened the door, which had been closed for jamming. Shakti Kitty darted in and lay on the floor. I returned to my spot flat on my back, and tilted my head in her direction. She immediately got up and pressed her purring head against my forehead and held it there... crown to crown, third-eye to third-eye, heart to heart. We marinated together in the palpable radiant vibration of love that the third activation had rendered in the space. The bliss was there. The tears were there. The divine benediction was there.

Needless to say, my life was forever changed by this series of heart activations. It illumined my entire being and the world in a new light... every step and every breath. I was walking around in a completely different, expanded reality. It still included the old one, but I was looking at it through a different lens. My baseline energy level and frequency had surged again and would take some time to integrate. Meanwhile, I was basically walking around in the blissfield in daily life, though still largely isolating as much as possible during the incredible unfolding of the awakening. It felt like I was a cup... full to just above the brim with divine bliss... and the slightest bump or trigger from life would cause it to spill out into the world of its own volition. The flight of a bird, a crashing wave, or a gentle breeze was all it took to overflow my heart and stream tears of joy and beauty down my face. Every drop that spilled was instantly replenished from its infinite source, through the miraculous door of the spiritual heart. It is here in this timeless, quantum source point where divinity and humanity unite in blessed communion... dissolving into each other and then flooding all of creation with its essence.

In addition to the physical and energetic transformational components, the activations would have a profound impact as a set of teachings. It was clear that Spirit was presiding over a bodily metamorphosis of some kind, but I also sensed that I was being prepared or groomed with a directed intentionality beyond my understanding. I had been gifted mystical, yet visceral experience of a range of emotions associated with love, gratitude, relationships, suffering, and compassion. Each facet had its own vibratory signature and could thereby be wordlessly felt and recognized. Coupled with the heightened recognition of all energies arising in my daily experiences, these heart activation teachings served to establish a glossary of emotional vibratory signatures that could be put into service. It would prove to be an important part of a healing toolkit, which would soon be employed as the mystical journey continued to unfold.

The Yellow House

AT THIS POINT in the awakening story, my daily grounding walks were among the most important routines in my life. What began as walks to heal and strengthen my physical body became essential to the balance and vitality of my changing energetic body. I felt the grounding embrace of the Earth the instant my bare feet hit the sand, and on days when I couldn't take my walk, I strongly felt its absence. Grounding in nature proved to be the most effective tool in stabilizing, integrating, and embodying the increasing vibratory currents flowing through my being. I would walk up the coast from my home beach as far as the tide would allow and back, usually doing three laps. I had a particular spot where I liked to turn around, about fifty yards past my favorite beach house on that strip... the yellow house. That is where this next story begins, flows, and ends.

It was my favorite house for several reasons. Most simply, yellow is my favorite color and it always drew my eye. There was also a kind, personable man who appeared to own the house and was often out on the deck. He would frequently wave and greet me warmly as I pounded that stretch of beach. Finally, there were three beautiful dogs that spent most of their time hanging out on the deck watching the action. The largest was an elderly yellow lab. He had some pronounced gray on his snout and some clear hip issues. He could no longer work off his ample meals and carried a few extra pounds. The middle-sized dog was a beagle with a rich, defined coloring and a low rumbling bark. In contrast were the piercing yips and yaps of the smallest dog, constantly running around in circles and on the move.

He looked like an oversized Yorkie, with long, light bronze hair. The dogs loved to greet me vociferously with sustained barking while I was in view, except for the old fellow, who would provide a single token bark as I walked by. I would lovingly greet them and always enjoyed our interactions when I passed by. They would take it down a notch on my second lap, and often ignore me altogether on lap three!

The story begins in April of 2019, shortly before Easter, and spans about two months. It had been a month since the last of the three heart activations, and I was feeling wonderful. For several weeks I had been singularly focused on stabilizing and integrating the higher frequencies of my energetic body. It was another beautiful day and I was gratefully grounding my bare feet in the loving embrace of Mother Earth. As I approached the yellow house I sensed a thick somber wave of energy throughout my being. It was like the sun was suddenly enveloped in clouds, though it shone brilliantly and unobstructed in the clear blue sky. I instinctively glanced up at the deck as I passed the house to look for the dogs, and was slightly disappointed that my friends weren't outside barking at me. That's when my eyes locked on to a profound scene in the large lower level picture window about fifteen feet from my path. The ominous feeling surged mightily again, and I found myself looking at its source.

There was a hospital bed pushed up against the length of the ocean facing window. A medical machine stood in the corner revealing lights and numbers, with a web of various lines and tubes connecting it to the patient. An elderly Asian man lay motionless in the bed, neatly tucked in, and with his head turned enough to the left that he could behold the beautiful coastal view. There were numerous pictures and cards adorning the walls, and a giant colorful Chinese dragon balloon hung from the ceiling above his head. I intuited that the man had been moved here to live out his final days in this beautiful setting. I hadn't seen him before, and thought that perhaps his family was renting the lower level of the yellow house from the dog owner.

At his bedside sat a woman, presumably his wife. She wore a traditional silk robe, had meticulously pinned and set hair, and an ashen white powdered face. She was stunning, and she sat equally motion-less. She too was facing the sea, but her eyes were attentively fixed on the man. She didn't appear to blink, let alone look up at the beauty... that was secondary. I was awestruck by her utter stillness and deliber-ate focus. The heaviness of her heart filled the coastline. I didn't dare stop or even slow down too much... even glancing up felt like I was intruding on a most intimate moment. Fifty yards beyond the house I would stop at my usual spot, say a brief prayer, and turn around. I walked by the yellow house again, and was presented a longer view due to the additional large window on this side. The magnetic scene and the powerful energy that was far too vast for the house to con-tain were mesmerizing. I watched the woman move delicately and deliberately, patting his forehead with a cloth, wiping his mouth, and adjusting his arm and the blanket. Her eyes were glued to the man the entire time... never rising to behold the immense beauty of the ocean, the brilliant sun, or the sparkling water. This most glorious beauty had aroused my own senses and drawn the blank gaze of the patient, but the woman never looked up... just served.

Upon finishing the last lap, I would have normally stopped and gone home. However, I was so impacted by the scene at the yellow house that I decided to make another pass. I felt compelled to of-fer some love, light, healing, prayer, or anything that may serve this somber situation. So with renewed resolve, I headed back up the coast for another pass, intent on helping in some way. I would fo-cus on generating and embodying as much healing light as possible, so as I walked by it could perhaps illumine the scene or emphasize my prayer. I recited little chants and verses along the way, breathing deeply, and radiating my loving intent as I neared the yellow house. I was both determined and serious as I moved through the still domi-nant "dark" energy cloud. The scene hadn't changed, and I passed by as planned trying to project healing energy and light. I knew instantly in the depths of my being that it was entirely ineffective.

When I stopped at the turnaround, I paused and beheld the glori-ous sun and ocean. My heart welled up with bliss, my eyes tearing from the beauty, and I knew right away why I had failed. I had gotten so serious about my mission, that I hadn't fully opened my heart. Trying to love is no substitute for feeling it deep within your heart. Do what you will, only an open heart can provide the space or channel for divine healing love to flow. My body surged with a boost of intense current, which I met with profound gratitude. Now the timeless, dimensionless blissfield was the vast ground from which the entire scene arose, dark energy included. I walked by… the man was still and his wife fixated on his care and her service. This time I felt a beautiful communion with every aspect of the scene, as if I was breathing with all of its elements… the house, the sun, the sand, the waves, the man, and the wife. I held my hands in prayer pose as I passed, glancing up at the unchanging intimate scene. Despite fifteen feet and a pane of glass, I felt as if I was in the room with them.

Once I was about twenty feet beyond their window, thankfully and likely designedly, it happened. I froze in my tracks… I literally could not take another step. While my left foot was in mid air, having had no previous related physical issue, a deep piercing pain went through my left foot like it was shot with an arrow. I couldn't place it back down, and struggled with my balance just to lower it to the sand without falling. The sharp pain was relentless and I immediately started to breathe into it. I was still fully engaged in the healing activity with the yellow house, which connection intensified when I stopped, despite the pain. I knew instinctively that Shakti had stopped me. The current beautiful expression of the blissfield was meant to continue in this particular way. My role was to stand there as a vessel for Spirit to serve her purpose. I acknowledged this, and told Shakti that I would stay and hold this sacred space in my heart as long as needed. I would not move until my glaring foot pain had completely dissolved. As an aside, although this didn't occur to me until the next day, it seems that my bizarre, stigmata streak during Holy Week had again manifested. There was the actual nail through the palm in 2017, the draining of fluid and blood from my left side in 2018, and now a mystical foot piercing in 2019… strange but true.

I stood motionless adjacent to the yellow house for a good twenty minutes, resonating with bliss and transmitting love and light. I was vibrating to the level I had experienced during the prior heart activations, although this time I could remain standing. The bliss was there, and so was the pain, and so was the dense sorrow emanating from the yellow house. I knew this was another "first" on the journey. I wasn't sure what was going on, but was not at all concerned. What I did feel in my heart was that I was supposed to be standing there. I was part of the action, but I was clearly not the actor... more the witness of the action of Grace, and a grateful vessel of her divine benediction. I breathed and flowed with the current, staring at the sun and its brilliant streak of dancing light across the face of the water to the shore where I stood. Eyes wide open, tearfully in the depth and fullness of the moment, I watched several green-hued orbs of brilliant light move from the sun to the surface of the ocean. One after another they followed the sparkling path of sunlight to the shore, moved through me, and then beyond. I felt incredibly blessed to feel the bliss of the energy as it passed through doing its work. It was a group event... the energy, the sun, the water, the shore, my heart... all playing a role in something larger than I could possibly comprehend.

I realized that the man lay and I stood, transfixed on the same beautiful scene. We were suddenly somehow together, both being inundated by the powerful rays. Though I stood there outside, I felt myself come into communion with his being. I offered my heart, and to my surprise, was able to share in his deep peace. I wept with joy. The heavy sorrow remained very present, but it was not his. It came from the woman at his bedside, and I would meet this energy later in the story. The man and I shared this beautiful, intimate space together for about ten minutes until I felt grounded again in my body. I checked in with my foot. The pain was gone. Just moments before, I was unable to take a single step, and now I strolled normally back down the coast towards my car. Waves of bliss caressed and escorted me while I wept uncontrollably with joy, awe, and wonder. Deep gratitude filled my heart as I walked and prayed for the man in the yellow house.

The episode stayed with me all day. When I lay on my couch that night, I knew that it wasn't an isolated event, but the beginning of some indefinite role I was to play in the end of this man's Earth walk. My head dropped to my left shoulder and I was lying in the same position as the man lay in his bed. In a mystical flash, we were again in communion, only this time I felt like I was in his body. At this point it feels relevant to reference the three heart activations from earlier in the year. Within the ecstatic bliss state I had experienced a variety of emotions energetically, in a way I never had before. They included love in relationship, deep gratitude, profound suffering, and boundless compassion. Each emotion had a distinct vibratory signature that I could knowingly perceive as it revealed itself in the vastness of the open heart. These prior experiences would help guide me through what was to come with the occupants of the yellow house. It is clear that the heart activations were a critical part of this story, and had necessarily occurred in preparation for the opportunity to play a role in this divine, collective healing.

When my head turned like the man and we connected, my left thigh began to quiver noticeably. I immediately associated it with the man's body and as a feature of our communion. There was a mystical merging, and I felt his peace as if it were my own. We were staring together at the bright sun of the morning anew... in this present moment, now as before, feeling the great love of its radiance and even the warmth on our face. We wept... I wept... we wept. Opposite of where we faced, a murky mix of emotions emerged out of the vastness. It was the wife, for whom I felt the man's great love. I raised my right hand up from the couch, to where she sat in relation to us, and placed it on the cushion. As my hand came to rest, the thigh quiver halted abruptly, and I felt myself move into communion with the woman. Forgive the necessary vagueness, but again, I was I... I was she... it felt like her emotions were in my heart. They were distinct, and I intuitively recognized them from experience. Right away I felt her deep sorrow, a profound sense of loss in its most raw form. It was not like something had gone wrong, but rather the inevitable facing and accepting of this challenging aspect of being human. It was heartbreaking and yet beautiful, for it had a depth to it that could only arise out of spending a lifetime together. This was the dominant emotion in her energy field, but not the only one, as I would soon perceive.

I dropped my arm back to my side, and was instantly back in the man's field, with his now familiar peace signature. Right away my left thigh quivered with waves of energy to confirm the communion. A brief aside about this phenomenon... from the equally accessible lens of the witness, I recall being amazed at how the physical body appeared to collaborate with this non-physical or other dimensional happening. I consider it more light shed on this greater universal truth: Everything that manifests in consciousness, no matter it's density, is tethered back to its infinite source of pure light. In its full flowering, the entire thread is meant to operate as a harmonious totality, thus expressing diversity in unity. In a human being, this flowering is awakening to and living ones multidimensionality. For now, it's just a synchronistic thigh quiver. We opened our heart together, and the peace revealed another sublime divine flavor. I recognized its distinct signature. The love and beauty in the relationship he shared with his wife was so joyful that no physical scenario, including his impending death, could dim its radiance. It was a beautiful peace that he could never lose, because he didn't have it. He was it.

For my own part, I should add that my body on the couch was vibrating with tremendous energy. The entire encounter was occurring during another ecstatic heart opening in which every cell in my body was palpably blissful. At the risk of being too repetitive, words do not suffice here. I was weeping audibly with joy as I experienced the range of emotions. The tears of sorrow and suffering were just mingled in with the joyous ones. It was so beautiful that I reached back up to the wife with a knowing gratitude and touched the sorrow field. The thigh quiver vanished and a most beautiful compassion emerged from her heart. It was genuine, pure, and had an unmistakable vibration. It poured out of her open heart and flooded the man.

Having been in communion with him, I knew that this profound gift of love and compassion was all that he felt from her, and it acted as an inexhaustible power supply to his peaceful state.

My orientation then switched to being beside the man in this highly energized field of love and emotions. He was there, and I, and she, and peace, and sorrow, and gratitude, and compassion. I lay tearfully in the blissfield, so grateful and blessed to be present in this rich moment. We all shared the space, and breathed together as one, and felt each other and everything in the field. I spent perhaps thirty minutes intending love, peace, and healing energy into the space, lighting it up until the sorrow field had dissipated into its radiance. Now only this peace, love, and compassion remained. The man and I were being nurtured and warmed from ahead by the beautiful sun over the ocean, and also from the limitless nurturing force and radiance of the woman's open heart. "Here we are," I communicated to the man, "peacefully lying between two suns." We could clearly perceive which of the two suns was more powerful. The physical sun, in all of its majesty, is no match for the divine radiance of the open spiritual heart. In future communions on our journey, this is what the man and I did together... lie between two suns… too beautiful for words.

After this magical, mystical day and night, my rational mind would frequently arise with its doubts… Did that really happen? Was it all in my head? There is no proof for the logical mind when it comes to the mystical, yet I could not deny my actual physical experience. My body was indeed undergoing some kind of a measurable transformation, and the otherworldly energetic vibrations and bliss states were visceral and real. Regardless of the doubts that would naturally and persistently arise, deep within my being was a knowing that required no validation. The living Truth stands on it's own, independent of our ability to understand it. I resolved that I was part of some healing operation beyond my knowledge, and that I would be in it for the duration with the occupants of the yellow house. I was blessed with the presence of this vibration and it was to be shared. Every chance I had, I would walk by the yellow house in prayer or with my hand on my heart, intending to add light to this situation until there was some resolution, or Spirit moved me to stop.

The Monday after Easter was my first opportunity to walk by the yellow house. Through my open heart I would offer the love of Spirit to that space and the love of that space to Spirit... offer itself to itself for the greater good. I did this nearly every day for a month, multiple passes per walk. Several happenings during this span merit a mention in our story. On that first Monday, as was the case on many a visit, the tide was in to where I could not get beyond the barrier that preceded the yellow house. I was caught about a quarter mile away. I went as close as I could and stopped to project love and light from there. This became my routine when necessary. That day I felt such a strong yearning to be closer, that I proclaimed to the Heavens my wish to deliver the energy more directly. Just then, the lone bird near me in that section of beach slowly took off up the coast. It flew only a few feet from my head, and as it passed, I reached out with my heart and asked the bird to "take this love to the yellow house." It flew straight over the intended divine target and my heart jumped! Bliss spilled into and out of my being as I stood there. "Oh, if only more birds would come and carry some more love," I thought. Right on cue from around the corner, about a hundred birds poured up the coast, over my head, and over the yellow house. I fed them all of the love and light that this heart could hold, crying with gratitude and awe of the synchronicity. And yes, this flight pattern probably happens dozens of times per day right in this very spot, but at this particular instant it was divinely beautiful and powerful. Of course, I wept! Why not... I've been crying for the last year and a half. In the blissfield, every tear is pure beauty... rich and full of life, no matter if it is caused by joy or sorrow.

The birdies and I would work together all month on the yellow house healing love team. Depending on the tide, sometimes we went together and sometimes the birdies delivered. A similar arrangement arose with the dolphins. They would often swim up the coast with me at my pace, radiating their divinely inspired love signature. If the barrier impeded my path, they would happily deliver my messages of love and light along with their own gifts. My connection with animals and creatures has been strong most of my life, so this was an especially joyful way to express my healing intentions and transmit love. In the context of my personal journey, I was continuously being healed and taught by every interaction. Spirit was revealing the true nature of my being and its connectedness to the rest of life. It wasn't me doing something, but rather a grand conspiracy of life pouring love into the yellow house. I was on the team with the birds, dolphins, water, and sun… everything is in on everything! This month of walks was paramount in stabilizing the higher frequencies that continued to move through me with growing intensity. I was now able to embody the higher vibrations and still function on a basic level, like going to the beach and taking walks. At first, the bliss bombs would leave me lying on the floor sobbing… absolutely delightful, but certainly not functional. Now I was walking around in a tolerable realm of the blissfield, with the power surges and tears of beauty ready to burst at the slightest provocation from life. Sometimes it felt like I wasn't even touching the ground, and I would tell my sister jokingly, yet seriously, that I felt loosely tethered to the planet.

The first time I caught the tide right and could walk by in person again, was memorable indeed. Noticeably, on approaching the yellow house, I didn't sense the dark cloud of energy. I was walking the openness of my heart into another openness. I simply felt the peace of the man. As I walked by the scene was unchanged, except for the color of the woman's robe. The exquisitely embroidered silk had been green and was now bright yellow. Nothing had moved, including the man in his familiar position facing the ocean. The woman was still, but her eyes were fixed on him attentively. Most notably, the heaviness of deep sorrow was gone, or I was no longer projecting it upon her, or both. After I had turned around and was walking back, I had my head down and my hands in prayer pose as I passed. To my great surprise and delight, I glanced up to find the woman looking directly at me. That was a shocking first! She smiled, joined her hands, and nodded respectfully. I stopped for an instant and returned the gesture, before continuing down the coast. The entirety of my being was overcome with that indefinable benediction. The bliss was there, and tears of joy emerged. When I took my second lap that day, there was a caretaker and a daughter in the room as well. I was gifted a solemn bow from the daughter on the way up and a smile and wave from the nurse coming back. About a week later there would be a son, and I watched the man's nurse tap him and point me out walking by with my hand on my heart. She was likely saying, "That's the crazy guy we've been talking about who walks by the window everyday in prayer!" Nonetheless, the son came up to the window and greeted me with a friendly nod and smile. The man and I were there. The peace was there, but the sorrow was gone.

Another afternoon walking by the yellow house was especially noteworthy. One beautiful day, on my first lap by the house, there was a large gathering. The room was full of about a dozen lively and smiling family members. It appeared that both the son and daughter had their whole families with them. There were grandkids climbing on the bed, photos being taken, and adults reuniting. It was lovely, and it filled my heart with joy. I did my typical prayer pass. On my second lap the entire family had spilled out onto the beach, laughing and watching the kids play in the sand. There wasn't much beach that day due to the tide, so both to and fro I walked right through the middle of the group, weaving between them, hand on my open heart. I was blessed to share warm nods, smiles, and hellos... spilling bliss everywhere. I felt a wonderful acceptance from the family, who had grown accustomed to my constant flashing presence. Whatever they thought of me, they were clearly very kind people. During this intermingling, the owner of the house waved me over and introduced himself. I was really excited when I realized that his three dogs were out, and I was formally introduced to my canine friends. The old-timer yellow lab's name was Duke, which was written on his Frisbee that was older than the other dogs. The beagle was appropriately named Buford, and little Mr. Yip Yap was called Chauncey. I eagerly loved on all three of them,

46

who were not barking at me for the first time in our newly budding relationships.

Twice during this six-week span I took a short trip. While away I continued to commune with the man in the yellow house every day and project love and light from afar, assured that the dolphins and birdies would make up for my physical absence. No matter where I was, the man and I would take our repose in the vast openness of the heart, bathe in the peace, and be nourished together as we lay between two suns. In the interest of the chronology of the larger narrative, I'll say a few things of note about each trip. Some of my experiences while traveling would figure prominently in the future unfolding of the awakening journey. I'll then return for the resolution of the saga of the yellow house.

In May of 2019, I visited family at home in Maryland for five days, three of which I spent at the barn with my stepmother where she boards her horse. While I had never formed a bond with horses before in this life, my recent heightened connection with the animal kingdom left me eager to explore this communion. On each trip to the barn, I would visit each of the ten or so horses individually, wherever they happened to be. I stood with each one and gently stroked them, pursuant to their comfort level with contact. I was essentially just breathing with them, sharing the silence, and expressing love and gratitude for their presence and company. It was beautiful, and I was quickly aware of and impacted by their potent energy fields. There was an awesome power latent in their stillness… and sometimes their not so stillness! After making the individual rounds, I would wander out into the middle of the field and stand by myself. I remained still, allowing for any horse to approach and interact with me as they willed. This produced many beautiful, blissful moments. The horses generally came for a loving touch, although one feisty friend solely and purposefully came to bite me! I formed special bonds with two particular horses, both of whom were struggling with a trauma on their journey. From that time forward, they would be included in my healing and prayer walks. My experience with the horses was profound and had triggered a deep familiarity in my heart, like a vague remembrance of strong bonds with horses in prior lifetimes. In any case, my longstanding resonance with Native American spirituality had been rekindled in the glow of the beautiful encounters with my new horse friends.

In late May of 2019, I drove to Sedona, AZ to hike in beauty for a week. I had never considered going there before, but now was feeling magnetically drawn. I needed a break from it all, so a solo retreat in nature seemed like a great idea. I was all about walking these days anyway. For the duration of this trip, I engaged in my remote healing practices and usual energy work. Multiple times a day, I would intend healing love and light to a growing list that included the occupants of the yellow house, some family members, and a pair of horses. I had researched some of the sites and phenomena associated with the area, and wondered how my heightened vibratory body would feel amid its noted vortexes and energies. I hiked the area for nearly eight hours a day for four days, and it was both healing and magical on many levels. The sheer beauty of the land alone was enough to keep me welling up with waves of joy the entire trip. On the first day I had a full bliss bomb under a motionless, hovering eagle while standing before the majesty of Courthouse Butte. Conveniently, no one was close by enough to hear my audible weeping. Somehow, I managed to keep my feet. Interesting, I noticed during my stay that I felt more energetically at ease, more grounded in my field than normal. It seemed that my heightened vibration was harmonious with the Sedona frequencies, providing a nice repose from the recent, radical fluctuations. There was a comforting resonance with the land, and despite the vitality of my energy field, there was a relaxing sense of peace... a welcome exhale on my rapidly unfolding journey.

I spent the last two days hiking in Boynton Canyon, where I felt a deep resonance and was profoundly affected. For years I have been seeing faces or beings in nature... in the clouds, rocks, tree bark, etc. It's one of the fun ways I play with creation. Here in this Canyon, life took our game to the next level, and nature came alive like never before. The stone people in the cliff faces, large and small, were so animated. I felt embraced by the land in such a magical way. I sensed the aliveness of every particle, each fully distinct, yet emerging from a single presence or consciousness. I traversed the paths and veins of the Canyon as just another particle in the great totality, with a new-found sense of unity with creation. I was highly energized and highly stable, walking around in the world. The bliss was there, and tears of joy flowed freely and often. I was filled with Spirit and that sacred Love that is both its origin and fragrance.

On several occasions while hiking through Boynton Canyon, I discovered what I'd call "Medicine Wheels" created in little clearings off of the main trails. Each time I was drawn to stop and rest, sharing the space with the energy of the Wheels. At one such sacred spot, I broke into a spontaneous chant, ceremoniously pulled out some of my hair, wrapped it around a small stick, and left it as an offering in the hub of the Wheel. While performing this task, and during all my steps in this particular canyon, I felt a tremendous sense of Déjà vu. I was certain that I had tread these trails before, lived among these glorious rock formations, and perhaps even carved some of these trails with my own feet. The Stone People were like old friends or ancestors, and I again felt deeply connected to an intuitive, yet unknown rich history of past Indian incarnations.

I returned home to Topanga from my wonderful trip and resumed my beach walks, eager to pass by the yellow house and lay eyes on my brother... the man in the window. I had left Sedona, but Sedona had not left me, and I would carry it with me from that day forward. The whole of my being was abuzz and I noticed the absence of the land's resonance. I was going through another phase of physical and energetic awakening symptoms, and felt the need for grounding more than ever. I pounded the sand with my bare feet daily and breathed in the intoxicating ocean air. Only now when I walked the beach, I had the entirety of Boynton Canyon and Sedona in my heart. I walked the canyon through the coast as if the entire coast was in the canyon... the canyon in me, me in the coast, the coast in the canyon... a surreal infinity loop of space, time, and energy pervaded consciousness.

On my first day back, the man in the yellow house lay in his familiar position, as if he hadn't moved at all, his head facing the ocean. One of the two caretakers with whom I have grown familiar sat at his bedside. The vibe was peaceful. I passed by in light-giving prayer, hand on heart, as I had been relentlessly doing for six weeks now. The nurse looked up and made eye contact with me each time I passed, greeting me with a warm smile and a gentle nod, as was her custom. The healing team was in full force... the radiant sun, the cleansing ocean, the giving dolphins and birds, the nurse, myself... all cradled in the vast loving embrace of Mother Earth. For the next several days the tide prohibited me from walking by the house, but I was there sending my love from down the coast as I was accustomed to do.

One day in mid-June, I arrived at the beach in good spirits and put my feet in the sand. I paused to take in the beauty of the ocean, filled with love and gratitude for the blessing of being alive. I was especially excited because I could see that the water was out far enough that I would be able to reach the yellow house on this day. As I stood there, a pod of about a dozen dolphins rose to the surface across from where I stood, and just stayed there... still. They were facing every direction but none were moving, other than bobbing with the motion of the water. I was awestruck by this, as I hadn't recalled this particular action or non-action before. They tended to always be moving one direction or another. I stayed still with them, for several minutes, before they began to head up the coast. They moved remarkably slow. In fact, I had to slow my walking pace to remain on track with them... It felt like the right thing to do. The dolphins and I moved in tandem up the coast about a half-mile at this slow, methodical pace. As we did, I felt an eerie tingle all over my body and the air became thick with a palpable somberness. I strongly intuited that something had happened and that I may be participating in a funeral procession of sorts. My heart remained open and I was lovingly resigned to the will of Great Spirit, come what may.

As we approached, at the house preceding the yellow house, the dolphins stopped again. They remained risen at the surface, not moving at all just as before, but now they numbered about two dozen. I froze in place with them and we remained there in that space together for another several minutes. The energy was saturated with a deep sorrow that I felt in every cell of my body. Somehow I was given the inner knowing that the man had died. My blissful heart allowed the sorrow and pain to be expressed and I burst into tears for all concerned, including myself. As I wept, I realized that I stood in the very spot that I had been frozen in place nearly two months ago when this mystical story began. A circle of life had been closed, punctuated by another magical synchronicity.

The dolphins and I continued our slow "march" up the coast. I glanced in the window of the yellow house as I passed, knowing tears streaming down my face… the man was gone, the decorations gone, the hospital bed turned on its side against the far wall, the medical machine unplugged, and the massive Chinese dragon balloon largely deflated. We continued to the turnaround spot just ahead, where the dolphins stopped again. I stopped too, and stared out at the ocean, watching my dolphin friends gathered at the surface, fins everywhere, forming a tight circle. They were moving within it, ever so slowly in every direction, yet never leaving the defined circle. In alignment with my recent experiences, I perceived that they had created a Medicine Wheel, and I was participating in some sort of closing ceremony. I was highly energized and the bliss was there, but I was quickly inundated with massive energies, like waves of emotion crashing over me. I felt the cumulative sorrow of all involved in this story, as a global field containing the family's grief, the wife's profound sense of loss, and even my own sorrow. The comforting and familiar peace of the man in the yellow house, that I had grown to love and appreciate so deeply, was starkly absent. He was gone. I cried openly, allowing the totality of the emotions to be fully felt. I wept then as I weep now...

It felt like five or ten minutes passed, though it also felt timeless. I breathed and channeled love and healing light through my heart, until all of the sorrow and pain in that space had dissipated into the blissfield. All the while I was heart-linked to the beautiful sacred Wheel of the dolphins. I resettled and somehow the dolphins spoke directly to me through my open heart. They thanked me for participating in this healing venture, for playing my role in delivering light to the actual physical scene, and for now helping to bring closure to the darker emotions enveloping the drama. It was absolutely beautiful, and my tears of sorrow became profound tears of joy, love, and gratitude. I raised my arms and head to the brilliant sun, feeling its powerful life force and gentle warmth. Then I felt the peace… the very unique vibratory signature that I knew to be the man's, and it was coming from the sun. After countless hours of lying between two suns, the man had become one with the sun in the heavens... perhaps just to say "Hi" or to radiate a little love on the yellow house.

My heart and body resounded with joy and love. I looked down at the Wheel and the dolphins were actively jumping out of the water all at once, in joyous play, exposing their full bodies. It lasted for several minutes. The bliss was there, love and peace filled the space, and the dolphins took off up the coast with my full love and gratitude in tow. I turned around and started walking back, full of joy, having processed and released the entire drama in its entirety. The story had ended. However one may view the manifestation of this tale, it was the truth of my experience. It was full of beautiful teachings, lessons, and revelations about the nature and power of love and healing. In combination with my two short trips, the story of the yellow house would spark the rebirth of my own Medicine Wheel, which would provide the structure for my future healing activities and multi-dimensional awakening journey.

The Medicine Wheel

WITH THE RESOLUTION of the story of the yellow house, my grounding walks had new life… same walk each day, brand new each day. There was no "feeling" around the yellow house. It felt just like all of the others on this strip of coast. The man's final room had been cleared and repurposed as a sparsely furnished sitting room. I felt great considering all that I had been through during the first half of the year, and was walking around with an inner joy and peace that was ready to spill out in an instant. The current was high, but I had seemingly managed to stabilize the new frequencies. During my walks I would greet the Earth and offer love, light, and gratitude from my joyous open heart. It served as my medicine walk, both for my own healing and growth, and for those whom Spirit had guided me to help. I connected in a unique way with each being that I served and remotely worked on each energetically… animals, family, friends, a stranger I saw on the street, etc. I constantly felt the love and light of Spirit, and noticed how it would well up or brighten in certain circumstances, often unexpectedly. It is quite an extraordinary situation to feel a "Will," other than your own, emerge within and act spontaneously.

The normal functioning of our will is typically dominated by our minds, based on what we think in a given situation and determine to be the appropriate action. Of course, the expression of our will is also often driven by our emotions. However, this may be deceptively less common than we think, as it usually occurs when the mind has decided to "follow your heart" this time. I am referring to something much deeper here... how Spirit expresses its Will through the heart, or what I call the action of the "spiritual heart." Only the open heart has the sacred space and vibration to serve in this manner. In my experience of this phenomenon, normal conscious awareness becomes the witness, and a spontaneous movement of Spirit occurs before any consideration to act arises. In this way, I see it unfold as it happens, just like everyone else. It is similar to "channeling" speech, hearing the words as they are spoken with no pre-cognition, as the language is sourced from a greater depth than the thinking mind.

At this point on the journey, the spontaneous arising of divine energy is occurring with greater frequency in my daily interactions. Due to my heightened sensitivity to reading situations energetically, I can usually perceive what Spirit is up to, but not always. Sometimes the energy just surges without warning or apparent reason. In this case I simply remain in resonance with the vibration and radiate its light, never knowing what divine magic Spirit was working... and this could be anything, because absolutely anything is possible. I'll share one such story involving the movement of this "divine will" in action.

On a Sunday evening in July, I stopped at the grocery store on the coast to pick up a few things on the way home. I was exhausted from my fifteen-hour shift as an audio engineer. It had been, and still was, a glorious summer day... about an hour of daylight remained. On my way into the store, I saw a man seemingly asleep or passed out on the curb next to the entrance. I instinctively tapped my pocket to see if I had any cash to spare, but I did not. Oh well, I thought, he's not even awake anyway. As I entered the store, several employees and the manager were exiting hurriedly, and I overheard them discussing an out-of-control, angry man causing problems in the parking lot. If they were talking about the guy I had just walked by, I thought, he seemed pretty under control to me. I did my shopping and exited the store. I was met by a wave of angry yelling! The man from the curb was screaming, "You wanna fight me? You wanna hit me? I will take you out! You will not touch me! I will crush you!" "The police are on the way!" returned the manager, ducking back into the store. I turned to my left and headed towards my car across the lot. There stood the angry man, just inches off of the store property, right next to my car, the only one in the area. He continued yelling angrily at no one in particular, perhaps at everybody. I was walking straight at him… I felt a few anxious butterflies of fear arise in my gut, but never broke stride. This looks like a potentially hairy situation, I thought, as I took him in.

He stood there mightily, maybe thirty years-old, about six feet tall, wearing blue jeans, shirtless, and red as a beet. I imagined he spent the day on the beach across the street, partying hard and getting burned! His eyes were completely bloodshot and puffy, like he had been drinking all day, crying, or both. He had at least a half dozen tattoos and his body was ripped, like he had spent significant time lifting weights. He flexed menacingly as he literally spit out his angry words. I walked on, breathed in love and light, and projected it at my tormented brother. Love was the only thing I knew that was more powerful than fear, anger, and hatred. As I neared my car, he locked eyes with me. He seemed irritatingly unimpressed with me, my Sunday blazer, and my long flowing hair… he had sized me up as a punk. He looked down at my shiny car, that my buddy at work had waxed during a shift break that day, and launched a huge spit of contempt on my hood. Somehow he missed, not that it mattered. He was staring me down with venom in his eyes. I opened the passenger door and ducked in to place my groceries on the floor, pausing a few seconds under that cover to avoid his glare. He stood there in silence, just a couple of feet away.

Before I could formulate a thought, my heart welled up and my entire body was flowing with high vibratory current. Shakti had arrived in full force. I instinctively grabbed a cigarette and lighter from between the seats. Yes, not all of my attachments had fallen away! I stood up and walked right over to him, face to face. We were both silent and projecting powerful emotional fields. Part of me was shocked at witnessing my sudden, spontaneous action. I was less than a foot away when I shoved the cigarette in his mouth with no warning. His gaze turned quizzical. He was still breathing heavily from his anger, but his arms remained at his sides and he allowed my action. I looked into his eyes, raised the lighter, and presented the flame. He puffed multiple times unsuccessfully because he was hands-free and his lips were moving the cigarette all over the place. His eyes were fixed on mine, and were revealing a growing frustration. "One more time brother," I said with a warm smile, "We've almost got it." He complied. It lit and he took a massive inhale and an even larger relieving exhale, our eyes still locked.

After a few seconds, his eyes softened and his entire demeanor and energy field transformed. He began crying uncontrollably, body heaving and nose running. He grabbed the cigarette out of his mouth, and said, "I love you" repeatedly, and powerfully embraced me, holding on as if he would otherwise fall. I held him up. "I love you," he cried out multiple more times. I hugged him back, repeating, "It's ok, you're ok, I love you, too." This went on for nearly a minute before he pulled back and resumed smoking, our eyes now locked together in a tenderness that I couldn't have imagined just moments before. We just stood there for a bit, each of us sporadically repeating our lines. He leaned in for more hugs several times until he finally stopped crying. I felt his mix of pain and suffering in my own heart, and a deep compassion overcame me. The bliss was there, under it all, rising up and filling the space. It was beautiful. Just then an older man, about sixty years old, approached out of nowhere and joined our tight circle. My new intimate stranger friend remained in his newly found relative calmness, looking at me to see how I would handle the new guy. I turned to the man. "Who are you?" I asked softly. "I'm his father," he replied..."Let me help you, son." He said. "Come home and let me get you some help... we need to get you some help."

"It's ok," I told my new brother... "It's your father and he wants to help. It's ok." His dad nodded affirmatively. My new friend embraced me again, declaring his love. I backed away a few steps, saying, "It's ok, you're ok, I love you, too." His dad stepped in closer. They shared a few words privately, hugged, and his father took his arm and walked him across the lot to a nearby van from where he had been watching the drama. A bearded man stuck his head out of the van window. It was clearly his brother, who soon stepped out, and the three of them huddled together peacefully. I saw several smiles emerge from their circle. As I got in my car, his brother pointed at me and offered a sincere smile and nod of gratitude. They were all embracing when I pulled out of the lot. I was steeped in joy, crying my usual tears of bliss, and amazed at the beauty of the scene that I both witnessed and participated in. I have no doubt in my heart that the unfolding events were both instigated and driven by the Will of Spirit within me, and I marveled at its divine power.

At this point, a new clarity had arisen. It seemed as if the disparate components of my awakening journey were integrating into a larger, harmonious totality... the teachings, the healings, the physical and energetic changes, the synchronicities, and the ancestral connections. Some greater structure was emerging... some coherent form, through which the mystical unfolding would continue. When the transcendent immensity of consciousness breaks through the physical form, it will necessarily express itself uniquely in each vehicle or body. For me, it was Medicine Wheel. It would serve as a mystical foothold on the path, and provide a template through which I could more actively embrace my new, evolving role. I would take a more empowered posture in support and recognition of this radical transformation, and stand with greater resolution in the Truth of my being as it was being revealed to me.

During the events surrounding the story of the yellow house, I came to understand that I had played a role in a Medicine Wheel guided from a more expansive level of consciousness. Now I would operate a Medicine Wheel. I would hold open this sacred space and engage in remote energetic healing work for those that Spirit brought before me. I would be even more active and more fully embrace my spiritual journey. I would rise to meet the "awakening" challenge, knowing full well that I was like a newborn baby who required much teaching and training. The beauty of the Medicine Wheel is that there is really no healer, but rather Spirit is healing everyone within the Wheel. I am facilitating the happening by holding a space open with energetic resonance. I may set an intention for someone or some out-come, but it is only Spirit in her infinite wisdom, that does or does not heal. One thing I had surely learned is that all healing was done by Spirit, Grace, Goddess, God, Shakti, Supreme Intelligence, Source Energy... or, whatever signifier resonates with you. Ultimately they are all just synonyms for Love... only Love heals.

The Medicine Wheel emerged while I was walking on my familiar sacred stretch of beach. I was reveling in the intimate Earth connec-tion of my bare feet in the sand, with my hands held together on my heart center. When I opened my arms in a widening embrace to hug the world, a tremendous presence and energy vortex emerged and radiated out like a sphere from the infinite center of my heart. The dolphin and Sedona Medicine Wheels vividly flashed in my minds eye, to identify and confirm the nature of this field. I was holding open and anchoring a Medicine Wheel, a tangible yet invisible struc-ture. I intuitively knew that I stood in the West and was looking across the circle at the brilliant opening in the East, the position tradition-ally associated with Spirit in many indigenous cultures. Through the East, Spirit in her infinite Grace pours healing love and light into the Wheel. It passes through the center, through my heart, and fills and empowers the sphere.

As I walked, the Wheel began filling itself in... I wasn't conscious-ly deciding on its content, but rather it was appearing in my mind's eye as a "vision." I looked across at the East portal, and to each side proudly stood my two new horse friends, serving as the gatekeepers. Remmy, with his psychological struggles, stood on the North side of the gate. Zara, with her physical challenges, was on the South side. This orientation would later prove useful when I brought people's essences into the Wheel for healing, helping me organize and or-chestrate the sessions. Then Shakti Kitty wandered into the circle and lay in the middle. She would serve as a protector or guardian of the Wheel, and could roam the center and aid in any healing as she saw fit. Crooked Stick, my favorite birdie friend from the shore, would also roam the center, limping around on her severely disfigured leg. She provided a great example of living joyously in the light with a physical challenge. Mother Earth was the ground of the Wheel, providing her support, nurturing love, and energy from below. Anchoring the Wheel from above hovered my motionless Eagle friend from Sedona, who had presided over one of my sacred heart-centered bliss bombs.

And so the multi-dimensional Medicine Wheel, through which I would offer energetic healings and prayerful intentions, was born… or perhaps reborn, as I mysteriously seemed to know what I was doing. That's quite a phrase… let me say what I mean by multi-dimensional in this context. It begins with the understanding that there are multiple levels or lenses through with we can perceive consciousness. This is obvious from our lived experiences. We are concretely aware of our physical bodies present in time and space. In the waking state we are constantly having experiences on the physical or phenomenal level. We also know that there is a non-physical aspect of our being. In the dream state, we are off having adventures in some kind of light body that is not subject to the normal laws of physics in the waking state. In deep sleep, our awareness recedes even further, into yet another "dimension" of our being which remains largely unknown to us. We are multidimensional beings, and though we are aware of and cycle through the above three states, there is much more of our true nature to be discovered. It is from these other realms that our deep intuition, inner knowing, and spontaneous insights come… commonly referred to as the "higher self" or "soul consciousness." The effectiveness of the obscuring veils between these states is dependent upon where one sits on the awakening path. As one's consciousness expands to include its higher aspects, the sense of separation diminishes toward an all-inclusive unity in which all are levels are connected and accessible to each other.

Now back to the Wheel. Obviously, the horses are in Maryland, Kitty lives down the street, and birdie is on the beach. Likewise, whomever is brought into the Wheel is living their life in their physical body elsewhere. All beings in the Wheel therefore, are higher dimensional or non-physical aspects of themselves, or what we can call fractals of their total being. I am the only one present in the Medicine Wheel in an actual physical body, and through my connectedness to my higher aspects, can serve as a bridge between the dimensional levels. My physical body anchors the higher dimensional space to the physical Earth and my energetic body manifests the Medicine Wheel that draws in the essences of the other beings. The healing work takes place in this higher dimensional level, in which other beings can manifest an aspect of themselves. That higher aspect can then transmit or otherwise express the healing session into the physical form.

From that day forward, this is how I would conduct my daily healing sessions. I would bring my awareness into the Medicine Wheel, which was in constant operation due to its "timeless" nature, and begin with an offering of love and gratitude while bathing in the grace of Spirit's radiance. Each time a being entered the Wheel, by either asking directly or by the guidance of Spirit, some unique spontaneous action would occur relative to their situation. It could be an energetic sweep, a concentrated sphere of light, a story, a teaching, a chant, a hand gesture, and an infinite range of other possibilities. They would usually start in the center of the wheel before taking a position around it. A beautiful mystical communion arose among all the beings present. We each experienced and supported all healings and lessons that took place, and shared in each other's breakthroughs and joys. We grew and healed individually and collectively. And yes, I do realize that this is all quite abstract, strains credulity, and is psychologically diagnosable! However, considering our subject matter, it is important to characterize this activity to provide a true window into the mind of the mystic. Outwardly, I am simply taking a walk on the beach. But inwardly, there is tremendous activity and vast energy at play in the subtle, multidimensional realms.

At the end of July, after a few relatively stable weeks, I was hit with another big wave of ascension energy. I was undergoing more physical transformations with their corresponding symptoms, and my energy was quite volatile. The dominant symptoms this time included light-headedness, insomnia, itching, and lots of intermittent ear tones. It would last a solid three weeks. In keeping with the established awakening pattern, the physical changes and angst would subside and the vibratory current in my body surged mightily. After all, that is the purpose of the physical transformation... to enable the vessel to contain and embody higher levels and vibrations of energy. To paraphrase scripture, you can't put the new wine into the old wine skin. You may have noticed that I just slipped in the terms "ascension" and "embody," some verbal giants in the spiritual scene! These are beautiful words with profound meanings in various contexts. Yet please note how I could have used any number of words in their stead to convey the meaning of this expression. As indicated before, the words are just pointers and we needn't get hung up on their limitations.

Now there would be several weeks of integration to stabilize the higher vibrations in the body. By the end of the summer I was feeling pretty "normal" and grounded at the new energetic level. The bliss was there, fully accessible and easily provoked by the smallest happening. This makes perfect sense since the smallest happening is as divine and beautiful as all of creation. Tears of joy were magically commonplace, blissful heart openings hit me like waves, and life was a sacred benediction. It was a lovely time. I enjoyed a smooth integration of the latest wave and a welcome little break to settle into it. Good thing, because I was about to get rocked! A rise in bodily vibration enables a more expansive perception of the subtler realms... a little more of the invisible world becomes "visible." Likewise, one is therefore also more "reachable" from those realms due to the closing gap in resonance. In turn, the resulting contact raises the vibration yet again, requiring additional stabilization... And so the process spirals forward. Essentially, as the vibratory floor of your body expands, so do the levels of the peak experiences or contacts. This is unending in the realm of form, however subtle, and how we are all just "-ing"ing along.

It's now September. In recent months I had taken to lying sprawled out on the floor of my studio. My couch was no longer providing the firm foundation my body desired, so I had cleared all furniture from the center of my small space for my new frequent activity. One day lying thusly in stillness, I was communing with the Medicine Wheel. The current seemed particularly high, but I was totally stable. Suddenly and mysteriously, I realize that I lay in the center of a greater, more expansive Medicine Wheel! I literally felt surrounded by supportive, energetic presences that were checking in on their blossoming disciple. I lay in the middle. This is a lovely way to illustrate how an awakening journey is part of an operation carried out by higher aspects of consciousness. Moreover, there is an exquisite personalized quality, divinely orchestrated and tailored to help guide the individual through the process. For my story, it was perfectly fitting to use a Medicine Wheel. With this now familiar mystical device, Spirit could direct the journey and represent the movements of various energies, Spirits, Guides, Angels, or any other of the unlimited diverse expressions in the vast immensity of consciousness.

My eyes were closed, and I lay marinating in the heightened energy. I was welling up with bliss, crying tears of gratitude, when I felt the physical sensation of something landing on my chest... akin to the weight of a cat. I opened my eyes for certainty, but nothing visible was there as I had already presumed. Something non-physical, however, was definitely there. I closed my eyes and a clear vision appeared... a large beautiful white panther. It lay peacefully and lovingly on my chest in the center of the Wheel. It identified itself as a higher dimensional aspect of Shakti Kitty. So, Kitty was in my everyday physical life, roaming the middle of my recently activated Medicine Wheel, and also in the center of this more expansive dimensional Wheel as a Panther! She was quite the heavy duty being, serving with me on multiple dimensions. My heart overflowed with love, peace, joy, and gratitude... these primary blissful vibrations that are both the source and fragrance of the divine flower that is the spiritual heart.

My body tingled dramatically in the presence of these higher energies and aspects of being. It was not totally unfamiliar, but it was ramped up significantly. Over the years, I have sensed energetic presences in my midst on several occasions, including feeling invisible touches and hearing my name called out audibly as if someone stood right next to me. Now Shakti Panther had identified herself and a Wheel of beings made their presences known. They were entirely beneficent, lovingly and diligently facilitating my healing and awakening process, yet their identities remained a mystery. I lay joyously in the blissfield of this Medicine Wheel in beautiful communion with life, and all sense of time faded into eternity. Eventually, my body settled and I opened my eyes. There sat Shakti Kitty, watching intently from a foot away from my head. I wondered how much of this mystical adventure she was wise to… perhaps more than I. Once my eyes were opened, she graced me with some sublime love, snuggles, and purring. More bliss… more tears…

I spent the better part of two days lying on the floor connecting to, communing with, and integrating this energy. On the third day I would have to pull off a work shift, which was getting increasingly more challenging, as things got more cosmic. When I returned home that evening, I would have the most profound mystical experience to date. In context of the larger journey, it could be considered the fourth major heart activation. It had everything that we discussed and described in the previous three events, and then some. This one was absolutely massive… higher vibratory levels were reached, new energetic connections emerged, and it lasted for nearly three relentless hours.

This most mystical day requires a brief set up to contextualize something that had happened earlier that afternoon, and that would prove relevant to what unfolded that evening. It was custom for me to always have a couple of dollars in my pocket in case anyone asked for help, like someone on the street or at a traffic light. As we all know, this is sadly, but necessarily a very common occurrence. In the event that I would not be asked for a few days, I would continue adding dollars to the offering. As it happened, I noticed on Saturday night that the sum had reached twelve dollars. Cool, I thought to myself, I've got to give this away tomorrow. It's a perfect Sunday offering, as the twelve dollars could represent the twelve disciples! In the afternoon as I headed from the Santa Monica work site to the downtown cathedral, I was stopped at a light and saw a homeless man on the sidewalk in clear need. This was my chance, I thought, so I opened my window to hand him my offering. He was completely passed out, sunburned, and filthy. I yelled loudly multiple times to get his attention, though he lay just several feet away. Miraculously, my last attempt roused the delirious man who was struggling to open his eyes, and he reached out his trembling hand. I successfully made the handoff just as the light turned green and continued on my way. I prayed that the twelve dollar disciples would provide at least a small degree of much needed comfort.

I got home Sunday evening after my monster day in predictable condition. I was physically and mentally exhausted from work, compounded by the fact that I hadn't slept much since "waking up" into the higher dimensional Medicine Wheel. I was spent, but the current was high and my energetic body was abuzz. At about 11pm, I was standing in the middle of the room contemplating bed and an attempt to get some needed sleep. Suddenly I was struck by a massive wave of energy that sent shivers throughout my entire body. I clearly felt the presence of the Wheel Spirits I had perceived several nights earlier. I raised and extended my arms outward, slowly spinning around in the center of the room, and audibly acknowledged the vast Presence in the space. "It's feeling awfully crowded in here," I stated, "Isn't it?" My body was tingling dramatically in and around every cell. Yet this vibration in my body was also clearly outside my body, and filled the space. I continued to rotate in this manner and asked directly for the Spirits to identify themselves… for the Wheel to further reveal it's multi-dimensional, high vibratory content. It would not disappoint. The oft cited verse, "Ask and you shall receive," took on a whole new meaning and demonstrated it's awesome power.

Once again, it seems appropriate to pause the narrative for a brief discussion. As the content gets more "out there," it gets more challenging to describe. Let's face it, contact with invisible entities and communicating with them is not the subject of typical conversation. To be clear, these are not new concepts or phenomena. The awakening of such latent human abilities has been discussed, investigated, explored, and documented in all ages of humanity by mystics and sages of all religions. Based on my personal experience of these matters thus far, I view it as such... As human beings, we are equipped to perceive and engage with some amount of life force in order to live. The vast source energy is filtered through the limitations of the vessel and all of its particular conditionings. These include genetics, culture, education, psychology, emotions, and what we call karma, to name a few. With this energy we operate our senses and navigate through the world. Our individual combination of conditioning factors, through which the energy flows, constitutes a personalized metaphorical "stream" of consciousness. Seen in this light, life is indeed a co-creation.

Much of our world is seen with the physical eyes, but much more is unseen. For example, we don't see the flu virus before we inhale it, but we certainly feel its effects in the body and don't doubt its reality. When a human being undergoes a transformative energetic awakening, more source energy is "perceivable" and more of the unseen becomes accessible. As our consciousness expands, our "stream" expands in breadth, and its flow includes a wider range of life's infinite vastness. We are still co-creating our reality, so our connection to Spirit is still filtered through the individuated aspects of our consciousness. Therefore, the manifestation of multi-dimensionality will necessarily have a unique expression in each being. One man's medicine wheel is another man's mandala, mantra, gateless-gate, or what have you. Considering this, the Spirits and Guides that I drew into the Wheel were of my own choosing and particular to my set of conditionings. I'd like to officially introduce the word "fractal" here, to mean a piece or representation of a beings consciousness. This allows a multi-dimensional being to be in multiple places or even all places at once. Most importantly, the fractal also contains the whole.

So the consciousness, though seemingly "fractured," is accessible in its fullness.

Ok... let's return to our narrative to see how such an awakening unfolded in my story. Back to my mystical encounter, where I stand within a Wheel of invisible Spirits, the energies causing a full body tingle and prompting my audible call for them to reveal themselves. I immediately turned to face the West, the position from which I manifested my Wheel, to see who had me in the center of their Wheel. My soft, open-eyed gaze beheld nothing, but when I closed my eyes, a clear vision appeared and an inner knowing of Jesus' presence emerged. I was utterly amazed, but it also made great sense. I spun around to face the East, left open in my Wheel as a portal for Spirit to flood in. There was Jesus again. The Alpha and Omega, at once in the West drawing in Spirit, and simultaneously in the East as the very Spirit and source being summoned. Of course, I thought to myself, as I considered the Christ attributed phrase "I am the light of the world."

I was aware of the miraculous and other worldly nature of what was happening, but there was also an undeniable knowing of the truth of my perception. I cannot explain the source of this knowing. I was filled with love and gratitude, and my entire body vibrated with ecstatic joy. The bliss was there, tears were there, and I struggled to remain standing. In an astonishing flash, the beings in the portion of the Wheel that I faced revealed themselves. In the North was my late father. Instinctively, I reached out my left hand to him, and my right hand down to my sister. She happened to be lying in the center of my original Wheel at the time for other reasons. The three of us energetically joined hands for several minutes, silently bathing in this reunion of sorts. Great love was being transmitted in every direction of this blessed connection and our shared heart was a sacred benediction. So far, I have referred to both my original Wheel and the higher dimensional Wheel I was awakening to. This Dad encounter clearly reveals the fallacy of that division. There is only one Wheel, it's various densities superimposed in a harmonious whole, and I was merely opening up to its higher aspects. It is much like our limited "streams" of life, expanding to include more of the thunderous river of consciousness in which our seemingly separate streams flow.

In the Northeast gap, between Dad and Jesus, is the presence of St. Francis of Assisi. I have long felt a kinship with this great mystic Saint and his legendary connection to animals. My own life has been blessed with many such connections and beautifully enhanced by those relationships. Our story thus far already prominently features animals. One such animal Spirit resides in the Southeast position of the Wheel... a mighty, snorting Buffalo. Traditional energies associated with Buffalo, including abundance, power, and sacrifice radiate from the center of this majestic Being. In the Wheel, Buffalo represents a vast stream of indigenous ancestral lines, including but not limited to my own past incarnations. Finally, this Southeast position serves as a portal to access various sacred lands and cultures, in particular my Sedona connection that was recently reestablished. Looking out from the Wheel beyond Buffalo stretches the vast expanse of Boynton Canyon, with the full power and presence of its history, peoples, and rock formations.

Not surprisingly, in the South position I have pulled in a fractal of Paramahansa Yogananda's consciousness. His divinely inspired lifetime, books, teachings, and efforts to reconcile Eastern and Western scripture, have been important components of my spiritual education and investigation. In the mysterious yet undeniable revelation of his presence, my hand stretched out from the center in love and gratitude, and I literally asked him to take my hand. Magically... mystically, he complied. My hand was turned up, palm facing him with fingers spread. Immediately I felt his invisible fingertips connect to mine, as if an actual person had done so with a flesh hand. A pronounced new tingle, with his unique vibratory signature, pulsed in my fingertips and up my arms. In the multidimensional space of the Medicine Wheel, he was able to make direct contact with my physical body using only his energetic body by the power and resonance of vibration.

I stood there for several minutes fully submerged in the energy of this connection. Of course, the bliss was there. For some reason, while touching his hand I audibly asked Yogananda if we had met before. He confirmed immediately, putting the words into my mind to speak aloud. I was speaking as him, yet was also there as a witness, hearing the words as they came out... "Yes," he said, "We met near Sedona in 1850 when you were a medicine man." I was flashed a clear inner vision of that life. I didn't see him there, but I saw myself as well as two medicine women of the tribe, huddled close together in friendship. I instantly recognized them as two souls that are also in my current lifetime. They looked entirely different, but I intuitively knew who they were. Yogananda confirmed the vision and the incarnation in the Sedona area. That was the totality of our interaction in the Wheel. As far as I know, Yogananda was not in a physical body in 1850, but he was very clear about the date. Perhaps being a medicine man as he stated, I had drawn him into the Wheel back then, just I have today.

I lowered my tingling hand from his withdrawing contact and dropped to the floor. I lay sprawled out in the middle of the circle, having collapsed in tearful bliss. I was awestruck by what was unfolding, both the vast current flowing through my body and the mind blowing connections being made. It was clearly a single, divine movement... As is everything, for that matter! I stretched out my arms over my head towards the West, and extended my legs straight toward the East, the energy of Jesus present in both places. As with Yogananda, I invited Jesus to connect with me. My request was met with remarkable physical sensations. I felt simultaneous pressure applied to both hands and both feet, as if he had grasped me with his hands at both poles. Like before, it was delivered energetically through a vibratory tingle with its own unique signature, yet miraculously still felt like flesh hands.

I have been quite liberal with my use of the word bliss in these writings, but with good reason. In my experience, it is by far the most dominant sensation in connecting to or resonating with higher aspects of consciousness. It is the result of embodying these energies, and at the same time, the very substance of the energy. It is the cause, reality, and effect at once. The bliss can be critical on an awakening journey, in the absence of proof or logic for all things multi-dimensional. Being dominantly tangible in the physical body, it is undeniable and can serve as a helpful validation of a process or experience. The rational mind is expert at trying to explain away the mysteries of life, but life in its fullness is nothing but mysterious, and resists all mental explanation. As does the bliss, which cannot be denied, adequately described, or reduced to a concept. As such it acts like a great doubt eraser. Doubts are many and often arising as the true nature of our being awakens, but they pale in comparison to the awesome power and vibration of divine bliss. Lower vibration energies, like doubt and fear, simply cannot be sustained in the high vibratory blissfield, and dissolve as quickly as they arise.

So I lay in the Medicine Wheel connected at the poles to Jesus' loving energy, vibrating with ecstasy in the blissfield. I could not express my gratitude enough, repeating, "Thank you, I love you," over and over again as tears of joy streamed down my face. I had never felt so blessed. Suddenly, the homeless man at the traffic light from that afternoon appeared vividly in my mind's eye… his miserable physical condition, the resigned despair in his eyes, and the deep sustained suffering in his heart. I felt it all in its fullness and then a profound compassion flooded my heart and being. It was so devastating, so real, and yet still immeasurably beautiful. I had an intimate communion with the man I had seen for about thirty seconds. I made a vigorous plea to Jesus to take all of this wondrous love and bliss that I was soaking in and give it to the man… fill my needy brother with divine love and peace. I adamantly repeated, "Please, give it to him," over and over. It was not that I was making a valiant sacrifice, for I knew that I could never lose or be separated from the divine blessing that I had been gifted. I just wanted my brother to be gifted, too, and to share in the radiance. Although, even if such a sacrifice was made, the bounty of giving is so rich, it would more than compensate. What happened next would serve to illustrate that very point.

As I set my intention on this man, pleading for Jesus' aid and projecting love and light through my open heart, the Divine Mother Mary appeared in the Wheel. She was a vaguely defined translucent pink color and emerged soaring motionless above the Medicine Wheel, raining love and grace down upon all. I thought of Eagle that hovered in the Wheel and she indicated that she was the bird, too. She poured her loving bliss down upon me. It was so beautiful and had its own unique signature, and I experienced a new flavor of bliss within the bliss. Somehow, the immeasurable fullness of Christ's presence was added to... impossibly so. It was the same bliss, yet totally unique in the instant... a wonderful paradox, one of many you will inevitably encounter on any spiritual journey of depth. As this happened, the Divine Mother made it clear to me that this was in part a response to my compassionate outreach for the man, and my willingness to give this greatest of treasures away for his well being. It was an act of love for a fellow child of God that moved Mother to saturate my heart with divine Grace. I thought of this divine moment when I later read the dialogues of St. Catherine of Siena, in which God declares to her that the truest way to love him is to love his children. Loving God is easy, relatively speaking. The answer to love is always love... love produces love... this is Truth in any dimension, for love itself is the very ground of all creation. And through the open heart, the human being can access, embody, radiate, and live this truth in daily life. Love is Truth.

At this point, I had been embodying this high vibratory rate for a solid hour, and felt a growing level of exhaustion. Of course, nothing in the universe would cause me to end this divine communion of my own will. I had learned early in the process to stay out of the way as things became more mystical. And inevitably, the greater the act of surrender, the greater the Grace offered. As Mother Mary's energy receded to the Wheel above, her Son moved above me from out of the West. He descended, superimposed himself over my being, and emerged from within. I literally trembled. My chest was heaving and my heart nearly burst with love, joy, peace, and gratitude. For at least the next hour, I would be in direct communion with Jesus. Through my voice came forth spontaneous orations, transmissions, downloads, and teachings. When particular truths were uttered, I could feel a squeeze from his hands on my feet as an emphasis or confirmation. When a sentence came out of my mouth wrongly, it would immediately self-correct, and again a foot pulse to confirm.

I will try and relate some of what he told me during this divine communion as it pertains to my awakening, as well as a few mind-blowing experiences that he was gracious enough to share. Much to my delight, he told me he had been keeping an eye on me all of my life. Periodically, he would enter the being of someone in my life and check in on me. He gave me two examples... he was once the twinkle in my grandfather's eye when I was a boy, and he was also present with Berkeley Tom when he put his hand on my heart when I was a young adult. He confirmed that a series of spiritual and mystical experiences were divinely orchestrated to further my awakening journey. He included the healings, the heart activations and even the magical story of the yellow house. He also said that he used animals with me due to my great love for them and the corresponding vibrations it produced. He added that he had done the same thing with St. Francis. I acknowledged the great Saint's presence in the Wheel. The bliss was beyond vast, from the minute cellular level to the borderless interstellar level. I wept uncontrollably, loud enough to be heard beyond the walls of my studio.

During the gaps between the transmissions, my own voice would break through. "Thank you, I love you... thank you, I love you," was all that I could utter, over and over again. "No," he said, "Thank you." I was stunned. He thanked me for a number of things directly, including the loving intent of the Wheel, a few specific healings, my role in the yellow house story, and the profound act of faith and dedication to see it through. As he spoke from within my heart, expressing his gratitude so beautifully, his presence in the East dropped to its knees and washed my feet. It was done purely with energy, but I was so resonant in the moment that I was able to perceive it fully, and feel it on my physical form like a gentle massage. Incredible bliss was there, and love and peace and joy radiated out of the Wheel, filling the Universe. It was an amazing display of love and humility from the glorious Master, during which he referenced Mother Teresa's beautiful life of service and compassion, and the orientation of her loving heart. He showed me Ramana Maharshi vibrating blissfully... as an earthly example that I would recognize of the awesome power of radiation. Jesus' words were eminently beautiful, but the power of his radiance was beyond beyond.

Again, I was clearly feeling the physical strain from maintaining this vibration for such an extended period of time. There were body twitches, various jolts and surges of current, and I kept losing awareness of my breath. It was all beyond my control. I knew I wasn't driving the action, and actually thought that I might not survive the ordeal. I wasn't concerned or afraid, but I really didn't know. I was fully surrendered to Spirit. "Thy will be done," I told Jesus. He acknowledged and assuaged my doubts completely, and held me in his vibration for even longer. The blissfield was gloriously aflame. I was in it, and it was in me. Tears were continuous. We lay superimposed in the Medicine Wheel, connected in the infinite core of the spiritual heart. "It is the center of you," He said, "It is the center of me." It is the center and through-line of all beings, dimensions, Medicine Wheels, and consciousness... as the one being that we truly are. All life emanates from the single shared spiritual heart. I experienced an amazing felt sense of union with Christ and all life everywhere. It was so beautiful, true, joyous, and brilliantly radiant. My heart was ablaze with love. "Do you feel it?" He asked. "This is what I felt when I said that I was the Light of the World." I could feel it in every cell, and I knew that this is the space in which such a statement could be uttered. In that instant, I was a living embodiment of that scripture. Jesus said that we were really one, all of us, and that the reason he didn't appear to my physical eyes was that he didn't want to give me any further cause to think that we were separate. That is an unnecessary, intermediate step and he wasn't "effing around with half measures."

As if that wasn't enough, the mystical, multi-dimensional

unfolding would continue full speed ahead. My body shifted into the shape of The Cross, and I was given a most spectacular gift. Jesus brought me into his heart, his very being, during his final minutes of that life, as he hung dying on the cross. He allowed me to feel and taste his heart and guided me through the journey. I had no feeling in my legs below the knees or in my arms beyond the elbows. They weren't numb. There was no feeling whatsoever, like they weren't even there. I couldn't even sense the contact with the carpet I lay on to the smallest degree. I did feel the textured grip of ropes supporting me just above the elbows. Clearly, my Cross experience began near the end of the grueling ordeal, and I didn't feel dramatic physical pain. Interestingly, I did feel a sense of relief that the worst was over and the end was near. It's like I entered the scene on a "relatively" relieving exhale. Thank you Jesus.

The energy flowing through me was tremendous. The vibration of suffering filled the field. It was an astounding combination of the personal suffering of a particular man in time, those present, and the global suffering of mankind in all times. However one views the deeper metaphysical meaning of the Cross, it was clear to me in that moment that Jesus was actually and literally suffering for everyone. I just mentioned how the various vibrations of suffering filled the energetic field. What field? The only field there is, of course… the bliss-field. There was an amazing presence of ecstatic bliss underlying all the suffering and entire, horrific ordeal. The bliss was dominant still, amid which everything else emerged. I, he, we hung on the Cross in bliss! Despite the high vibration of the energy, I could feel my physical body failing. My breath became increasingly slow and shallow, and I sensed it wouldn't last much longer.

The next part of the sharing was exquisitely beautiful, intimate, and healing. I sensed a deep sorrow in our heart. He said that the most difficult aspect for him as a human being was letting go of Mary Magdalene, who was his wife. We wept. "She was my Ocean Girl," he said, as he shared his profound love for Mary. That simple line referenced and surfaced the deepest emotional block in the heart of my being, which I didn't even know I was still holding or denying. We felt our love together, released it together, and healed together. It was a beautiful cleansing. Jesus was healing me and teaching me profound truths at once. This place through which we are connected to all life everywhere, the spiritual heart, is a beautiful aspect of the teaching and meaning of the Cross. It marks the nexus of union of the vertical and horizontal dimensions of life. It is where and how the flesh is made divine... how the transcendent, divine light of the vertical flows into and fills the manifest world in the horizontal field of time. In the human physiology it is where the Immaculate Conception occurs... where the emergent Holy Spirit gives birth to Christ Consciousness in your heart, and where the presence of God awakens in you... as you.

My cross experience would conclude as remarkably as it began. I lay on the floor in the center of the Wheel, Jesus within and without, hanging on the cross in physical and emotional exhaustion. After a silent, solemn moment, my mouth opened and Christ's words spilled out, "Forgive them Father, for they know not what they do." The space from which these words arose, and the corresponding energy, was divinely beautiful. The blissfield was in full radiance and a deep love and gratitude poured out of our shared heart. A sliver of this love seemed like enough to heal the world. I felt a profound compassion for those who had put him to death. He directed grateful heavenly love towards them, as he considered their roles in this divine unfolding to be of no lesser value than his own. "It is finished," we said together, feeling the breath fall away. The all-pervasive vibration of Love had an incorruptible purity. There was a knowing appreciation and recognition of the glorious result of planting the divine redemptive seed of the Cross into the consciousness of humanity.

I was off the Cross. I lay in the Wheel vibrating in blissfield, tears continuously streaming down my face, as the multi-dimensional episode eclipsed the two-hour mark. I felt blessed beyond any measure. Jesus was still there, inside and out, and after relaxing for a few minutes we continued our communion. He began to speak about my life purpose. I was delighted, for I knew that this awakening journey had a greater purpose, and I yearned to live in alignment with the divine Will. My most earnest prayer was that my life honor the glorious blessing gifted to me. It was a perfect message... specific enough to guide me on my personal path, and general enough to be his wish for all of his brothers and sisters. The primary mission was simply this... to radiate the divine love of God in the world. That's it. Radiate and release, without concern for what the radiation produces... "I'll take care of that," Jesus declared. In my heart, I knew this already. When one loves unconditionally, one has an endless supply of love to give. As each drop spills into the manifest world, Spirit is constantly refilling you from its infinite source. Love begets Love, and the cup of the spiritual heart overflows with the Living Water from the bottomless divine well.

Regarding my personal path, Jesus acknowledged the Medicine Wheel and encouraged me to continue to intend healings in its sacred space. I could feel his delight with its creation, and my heart soared. He then asked that I serve the expanded Wheel that I had awoken to. I was the only aspect of the Wheel in an actual human body on the Earth. As such, I may be called upon and utilized when needed... In this healing expression, I was the feet on the ground. The divinely orchestrated Wheel would either send beings to me or instruct me directly about who, what, and where to act. As for my role on the healing team, he described it like this... find a crack, sliver, or opening of any kind in the heart of another. Plant a seed of divine light and love, using any and all of the tools and skills gathered in life. Tell a story, sing, share a teaching, listen, radiate in silence, etc. I am to find a way, by any act or means of a loving heart. If there is no "opening," the job is to lovingly facilitate one. And then, always and immediately, surrender the result back to the Wheel, to God... to that "Great Mystery" that is the ground of being.

Finally, and much to my surprise, Jesus gave me a direct mission to go into the world and perform the very next morning. He instructed me to go see a woman I know, who works in town nearby, and deliver a message to her from him. It was five brief phrases and he made me repeat it three times in a row to make sure I had it exactly right. Then I was to touch her heart center with my left hand while my right hand was on my own heart, as long as feels right. He added that this was how he wanted me to do a physical healing transmission for him when he asks. "It will be done," I responded, "Thank you, I love you." In our final moment he communicated that he loved my adjusted versions of "The Lord's Prayer" and "Hail Mary" prayer. "Really?" I mused, "I edited out a lot of your words!" "These are different times," Jesus said, "We're not effing around!" Then I heard him say, "Twelve, twelve, twelve, twelve, twelve" …loudly at first, and then fading out progressively toward the unreachable circumference of the Medicine Wheel. The bliss was there, and tears of great joy and gratitude spilled into the world. I took deep, relaxing breaths until I felt myself solidly in my physical body and sat up on the floor. It was 1:44 in the morning… nearly three hours after the mystical events of this night had begun. I have said this before and will likely say it again on this exquisite journey, but my life was forever changed. It could never be the same. That was not possible. I was transformed. The bliss was there.

The Table

ANOTHER NEW CHAPTER of life would begin the next morning. Energetically, I was lit up. The profound multi-dimensional experience of the prior evening continued to resonate throughout my entire being. It would take some time to stabilize and integrate the vibratory energy of opening up to more expansive aspects of consciousness. You have likely noticed the cyclical use of a few words commonly associated with the subject of spiritual awakening, such as activation, stabilization, integration, and embodiment. While they provide a loose framework for the larger arc of the narrative, they also correspond to patterns that emerged in the various individual stages of the transformation. While it is of value to consider how these processes unfold sequentially in time, a fuller understanding is that they are all operating simultaneously to various degrees in every moment. They are part of a single movement that is always ongoing in the living present of every human being.

Of course, you may be wondering... what about the mission? In the blissful state of my Jesus connection, I had eagerly accepted a divinely inspired mission. Upon waking the next morning, I would have to face the reality of actually carrying it out in the real world. Could I actually approach someone and tell her that I had a personal message from Jesus? Was this some sort of test from Spirit of my willingness to play a role in the multi-dimensional Medicine Wheel? Was I really "all in"? Yes, yes, and yes. I had been up most of the night in mystical awe and wonderment, and had been fortunate to manage a couple hours of sleep. I was physically and emotionally spent, but there was no returning to sleep after I awoke. The mission was foremost on my mind and I would not be able to rest until I faced it, one way or another. It must be acted on or denied. I made a cup of coffee and sat still, trying to center myself. I breathed rhythmically to settle into my body and bring more harmony to the surging flow of current. I was able to get so-called "centered," but it was the center of a maelstrom of anxiety and doubts. All the perfectly rational reasons for not delivering Jesus' message convincingly swirled around in my head, but they would ultimately never be able to overcome the single reason to carry out the mission. I had promised Jesus directly just hours earlier! This is where the rubber meets the road when it comes to free will. I'm free to follow what I perceive as the divine will or not. It's not a test in terms of succeeding or failing, but rather a gauge as to my earnestness and commitment to the awakening path. Was I fully engaged, sufficiently ripe to take this next dramatic step? There was no judgement looming, either way. God is eminently patient and loving towards his children as they journey back to source. I decided that sitting around was not going to be fruitful, so I would simply go for it.

I packed up my beach bag to go for my daily grounding walk and headed out the door. Within two minutes I was at the quaint little flower shop to do the deed. The owner was busy with a customer, of course, so my plan to avoid waiting was quickly thwarted. It is a tiny shop, so I sat down in the chair outside the stand where the apothecary and herb section was displayed. As I sat down I buried my head in my hands, thinking that the last thing I needed was more time to talk my self out of this. I raised my head and my gaze landed on two jars right in front of me. One was frankincense and the other Myrrh. Amazing! Spirit knew that I was struggling and provided this timely synchronicity to put me at ease. A surge of bliss welled up in my being and all was well in my heart and soul. Tiny miracles in life, if noticed, can have such vast effects. I would wait for about ten minutes, feeling reassured and ready to act.

As it happened, it went as smoothly as one could hope. Her customer stepped out, and I stepped in. "What are you doing here?" She asked with a smile. "This may sound totally crazy," I began, "but I had an outrageous mystical experience last night, and I have a message for you." She interrupted me right then, put her hand on my shoulder, and said, "Don't worry, I've channeled multiple times in the past. I understand." Now fully relaxed, I said, "Wonderful... I have a message for you from Jesus!" We stood facing each other, hands joined, and I carefully delivered the five brief phrases. I repeated the message a second time. I told her that he also wanted me to touch her heart. She allowed me to put my left hand on her heart center, while my right hand was own my own. We stood like this, breathing, eyes closed, for maybe thirty seconds. I lowered my hands and opened my eyes. She was silent and tears ran down her face. "I'm gonna go now," I said. I told her I loved her and she replied in kind. After a hug, I got in my car and headed for the coast. The bliss was there. I wept with joy from the sheer beauty of the moment, the miraculous unfolding of my journey, and the blessing of being alive.

I began writing these pages just a month after the mystical events surrounding the revelation of the multi-dimensional Medicine Wheel. Though my status was rather ambiguous at best, I was at a place where these writings began pouring out. Like this entire story, it wasn't a function of personal desire at all, but a movement of Spirit to further the unfolding. It is just a point on a path of expanding awareness, towards the discovery of the true nature of consciousness and humanity's relationship to it. The "-ing" in awakening is timelessly present in the field of time. Just like yours, my path will continue to uniquely unfold. After the multi-hour high vibratory connection to the Wheel and associated Spirits, my base energy level had surged from the prolonged resonance. I would need to anchor my body with the higher frequencies. Another period of stabilizing and integrating ensued, as per the pattern. Throughout the entire process of physical changes to the body, grounding has been among the most critical tools in stabilizing myself. I hit the beach hard and pounded the coast with my bare feet in the sand as often as I could. It was my 'go to' medicine, and was helpful as always. However, now it didn't seem to be enough, even when I significantly lengthened the walks or added a second full grounding session. The current in my body had reached new heights and intensity, and I was aflame with energy. I struggled to sit still, let alone get any sleep.

It is clear that the vibratory gap, between the normal third-dimensional density we are accustomed to and the higher dimensions I had resonated with, was quite vast. I began to realize that in order to be stable, I had to consider "grounding" in new way to accommodate the expansion. It was no longer sufficient to be anchored at one level, from which new levels could be experienced. The journey had progressed to where there could be just one level, with an expansive frequency range that is totality of perceived consciousness. I was a multi-dimensional being, and would have to be grounded in multiple dimensions simultaneously. I decided that in addition to my normal grounding Earth walks, I would also ground myself in the multi-dimensional Medicine Wheel. This is essentially being still, tuning in, and surrendering myself to the Goddess, that She may do her work. Happily, I found it very effective. My energy field would stabilize from this consistent routine. The base vibration level remained high, yet my being would find a harmonious repose. As a result, there was a further integration of the various frequency levels that I had experienced so far on the journey. One such grounding session led to a beautiful reunion and healing that I will share.

I lay on the floor in the center of the Medicine Wheel and relaxed my body. I proceeded with an effortless, rhythmic breathing as usual. The physical form and energetic body came into harmony and I fully surrendered to the multi-dimensional space. My heart was open and vast, and I felt a deep connection to all life. The bliss was there and the entire space was a divine benediction. I addressed the Wheel and the Spirits that could perhaps be considered my 'guides' with great love and gratitude. I repeated my customary refrain, "Thank you, I love you. Thank you, I love you." My heart spilled over with joy and my body tingled with bliss. Tears of beauty flowed like rivers. As an aside, please do not be lulled by the repetitive flowery refrain used to describe this mystic state again and again. It is ever new, infinite, afire, and more radiant than the Sun. I lay in the Wheel, supported by the loving embrace of Mother Earth, marinating in this blissful, healing communion. I was so enjoying the physical sensation of breathing and felt extremely blessed to be an embodied Spirit. I realized that I was the only being in the Wheel that had an actual physical body, as far as I knew. I then invited any Spirit in or around the Wheel to join me in my body to experience the glorious physical sensation of breathing, should they care to. "I assume it's been a while since most of you were in a body," I stated. "I have no idea of what you can actually feel in this scenario," I offered, "but it must be something, and you are most welcome!"

Instantly, my grandfather who had never previously been perceived in the Wheel, appeared in my mind's eye with a big smile. He spun around and descended until superimposed with my body... so beautiful! We proceeded to take a half dozen full, deep, invigorating breaths together. Then I sensed a tangible sorrow arise within the blissfield. There was a clear knowing that it was my grandfather's deep sadness at dying young (he passed in his early sixties), and his feeling that he didn't accomplish what he wanted to do in his last embodiment. My inner knowingness was coming from the fact that I was actually feeling this in our shared heart. There was no separation between us, so I therefore knew the source of the sorrow. I acknowledged and felt the sadness, and then projected great love and light into our shared field. I assured my grandfather that I knew the cause of his sensation of sorrow was a misapprehension. I've been alive while he has been gone, and I knew with certainty that the profound, beautiful impact of his Earth walk was not lacking. It was vitally alive in all of his relations, as present as ever, and still growing in beauty. The sadness dissipated into the omnipresent blissfield. A beautiful clearing and healing had graced the Medicine Wheel.

My grandfather left in a flash and immediately a childhood friend of mine, who had died in his early twenties, appeared for the same reason, seeking a similar resolution of a lingering sadness. I responded in the same manner until the blissfield was again pure and free in our shared heart. These were deeply beautiful experiences, in both the touching reunions with these wonderful souls, and the opportunity to facilitate healings. I also include this particular story because it was a new kind of healing for me. Rather than working with a living being, I was called upon to help a disembodied spirit for the first time. A physical being can seek healing from a spirit, and a spirit can seek healing from a physical being. In a later session in the Medicine Wheel, my grandfather would make himself known as occupying the Southwest arc of the Wheel, initially not revealed. Just to fill out the final Wheel position, Mary Magdalene revealed herself to occupy the Northwest arc during the same magical, mystical session.

The new practice of daily grounding both in the Wheel and on the Earth had been very effective in stabilizing the higher frequencies. While the transformation had been fierce, rapid, and relentless, I felt great overall. From my perspective, I was flowing along with the extraordinary phenomena of expanding consciousness, and my body was holding it's own amidst the rising current. Since the nadir of my medical condition and heart surgery, I have felt progressively healthier. In fact, I was quickly feeling better than I ever had in the past. Since the energetic awakening, I have had the strange sensation of growing younger, though that is in some measure a reflection of a less than ideal vitality from the outset. As I sit here today, I do indeed feel healthier and younger than ever... reborn, if you will.

A few other phenomena merit a mention in describing my current state or condition on the path. Firstly, my ability to sense and process energy has been dramatically heightened. This includes the energy fields of people, places, situations, potentialities, and unseen entities. I regularly sense the emotional fields of others, and with some attention, I can connect deeply to these feelings in my own being. This sensitivity to energy can be difficult to navigate at first, but its implication in the context of healing, is exceedingly valuable. It can be easier and faster to get to the core of a dis-ease in this immediate, non-verbal manner.

Another prominent facet of the awakening journey relates to the receipt of information and access to vast intelligence... what are often referred to as "downloads" in the spiritual lexicon. I have mentioned this phenomenon before, but it merits a little more attention here. I can speak only from my own related experiences, in which they have generally presented in two ways. The first one is getting the totality of information on a subject matter in an instantaneous flash or package. The understanding is total, but I can then 'open' the package with my mind and verbalize or process it fully if inspired. Quite literally, it is like a flash-drive of information whose files I can now access. It is a gift from the timeless that one can open in time... just like a human life! I have been experiencing such downloads more frequently of late. Often it's a teaching or lesson, but it can also be related to a presence, energy, or situation. I will suddenly understand something in its fullness... the cause, the current scenario, and the likely outcome of a given action. Of course, we all experience intuitions along these lines to some degree all the time, but they carry a certain vagueness that the "download" does not... The download is not suggestive, but rather informative.

The second type is like the first, but it unfolds in real time like a more traditional channeled communication. In this scenario, I am the instrument of vocalization and the detached witness at the same time. The words spontaneously flow out in my own voice without any forethought or formulated intention. I am hearing the words for the first time, having no idea what is coming next. As an appropriate example, many passages in this book flowed out in such a manner. There is a clear knowing that the thinking mind is not the source of the expression, but rather what can be called the "Universal Mind." As with most mystical matters, many well-known spiritual terms are associated with such transmissions and channeling, including connecting to the Akashic Records, Higher Self, or Supreme Intelligence. I feel it important to note that in all cases that have arisen in my personal experience, the vast intelligence or information emerged from within... never from without, whether it presented as directly from source or an individualized soul expression.

An additional effect of the awakening process relates to the functioning of memory, which seems to be evolving towards a new tendency. Rather than simply remembering an event or detail as from a list, my consciousness is drawn to fully re-enter an event or story to thereby see and even feel everything anew. Simply but abstractly stated, a non-linear aspect of consciousness can relive or experience a previous now moment in the current now moment, including the emotional content. In fact, that is how I documented the various stories in this book. With only little delay, I relived them onto the pages of my journal... I could see all the events unfolding anew, along with the corresponding feelings. Being inserted back into the scene at this depth, I simply put my pencil to the paper and the stories flowed back out with impressive accuracy. When I wrote words like "the bliss was there," or "tears of joy flowed," it was true in that instant as it was when it happened in the story.

It is my sincere hope that narrating the stories in this manner will somehow allow greater access for the reader to share a deeper sense of the unfolding events. In my own experience reading the works various sages and mystics, I have perceived the intangible energy and power that is magically imbedded within the words on the page when they have been sourced from higher states of consciousness. It is a form of vibratory transmission that cannot be otherwise created or emulated. Were you to sit in silence with Ramana Maharshi, you would have the opportunity to tangibly feel the energetic power, or Shakti of his presence. That very Shakti is also present in the words expressed from his heart, whether oral or written. May the Goddess so bless these pages, and leave her vibratory Grace for those with hearts ready to receive it. Whether we are living, writing, or reading these mystical tales, let us maximize this opportunity together by fully entering the narratives with open hearts and minds. Regardless of whether they are deemed reality or fantasy, stories are a magical way to communicate ideas, lessons, and human experiences. There are many in this book, which is itself one longer narrative. In that light, I will close this section with one more healing story. It reflects the current status of the awakening journey, the continued flowering of the Medicine Wheel, and highlights some important universal truths about healing in general.

This story literally hits close to home, as it involves family and the events described here culminated quite recently as I write this section. It really begins in May 2019, when my sister entered the hospital during her pregnancy for a blood pressure issue. The concern was for any effect this may have on my niece in the womb and the timing of her birth. At that time, in an effort to help or add light to this situation in any way I could, I held my niece in a healing space. The Medicine Wheel had not manifested yet, so I just held her essence close to my heart wherever I went and sent her healing love and light. She was a lovely addition to my beach walks. Shortly after, the Wheel emerged and I brought her into that space. We were already in beautiful communion, so rather than taking a position in the Wheel she remained attached to my chest and tethered to my heart. She had a rocky, relatively premature entry into the world. I say relatively because God's timing is always perfect, and premature is an arbitrary human term. She spent two stressful weeks in the NICU upon arrival, but stabilized nicely and adjusted to life in her new home.

Several months later, during a routine doctor's appointment, blood work revealed some troubling numbers. Her iron was significantly low, and her Hemoglobin count had plummeted to 5 from the normal range of around 12. She was admitted to the hospital for treatment and to diagnose her condition. She would undergo several blood transfusions. A large mass was found between her heart and spine in addition to some other abdominal anomalies. My primary healing activity with my niece consisted of lying in the center of the wheel with her on my chest, connected at the heart. We simply breathed healing light and energy in and out of each other in an infinity pattern loop. I would often trace the figure with my actual hand while we breathed to emphasize this flow. Additionally, my niece was enclosed in a Vesica Piscis... a foundational shape in sacred geometry pulled from the Flower of Life pattern, and used throughout the ages to indicate one's divine nature. The shape was being flooded with the light and grace from Mother Mary above, while Mother Earth below lovingly received and dissolved disharmonious frequencies. The posture towards the disease was always loving, honoring its arising and welcoming its dissolution, where it would achieve its greatest glory in highlighting the divine healing power of love. The orientation was one of gratitude towards the disharmony, never resistance.

I involved the Spirits of my Indian ancestry to take a key role in this healing. The Sedona stone people and rock medicine healers seemed like a natural fit for this particular situation. They were the mineral specialists in the Wheel and would offer their services to help bring my niece back into balance. "We've got to get this number (5) up quickly," I entreated. Their cosmic energy flooded the space of the Wheel through the Buffalo portal and turned the infinity shape of our breath pattern on it's head, revealing the number eight in bold, dramatic fashion. The eight remained prominent in my vision until I finally acknowledged the message that her number would rise to eight, in the space of a day as I interpreted it. Shakti would confirm energetically. Quite hesitantly, I shared this positive Wheel prognosis with my sister. She was naturally anxious and afraid regarding the health of her baby and the dire possibilities addressed by her doctors. I admit that I was worried about providing a hard number, as should it not come to pass, it might reinforce the darker potentialities. But it felt like the right thing to do, so I followed my inner guidance and boldly proclaimed the good news.

In thirty hours, my niece's number rose to 8.6, before settling back to an even 8. This result produced a needed wave of relief in the family and a brief respite in this ongoing, harrowing drama. This early development would prove valuable to the later unfolding of this healing effort in several ways. Most obviously, there was the immediate and positive physical effect on her body. Equally important was the establishment and strengthening of belief in a set of high vibration potentialities and positive outcomes. This was a critical part of my Wheel sessions with regard to helping others deeply impacted by the illness. I was consciously maintaining and emboldening this field of "positivity" that others could resonate with, connect to, or be guided toward. However it happened, and for whatever reason, I was elated. I expressed my deep love and gratitude to Spirit.

While working with the Wheel I asked Spirit directly to be shown what was going on, if there was a serious problem, and if so, where in the body. I received a very clear message and sensation that she was in "no danger," and was shown a vision two graphs. They were two sine waves that slowly decreased in amplitude (height), and then each leveled out to extended straight lines. They were representing the consciousness of spirit settling into embodiment in newborn babies. The top graph was labeled normal, and the crests and troughs of the wave were a given height before resolving to flatness, indicating stability. The lower graph represented my niece, and the height of the peaks and valleys of the wave was noticeably greater, before stabilizing like the top graph. The difference of the amplitudes at the start of the graphs indicated that my niece would have a more tumultuous entry stabilizing her embodiment. However, the extended straight lines arrived at simultaneously on each graph represented and reinforced the "no danger" message. There would be a normal stabilization into her physical body, but she was in for a wilder ride at the outset.

That was the totality of the message, and I would not receive more specific answers to my questions. I acknowledged the transmission with gratitude, and despite my brotherly concerns, the Wheel was literally all smiles. Of course, it was a very serious and potentially deadly situation indeed, despite the favorable vision. Her team of dedicated doctors had other, less positive things to consider. It was their job to test and prepare for a wide range of serious potentialities, and their best guess was likely cancer. Additionally, due to the perilous location of the mass, just performing a biopsy to find out would be a quite dangerous operation. So there was an established set of darker, lower vibratory, fear-based potential outcomes.

In contrast, during my ongoing healing sessions surrounding my niece, I maintained and nourished a higher vibratory, "no danger" outcome. In this potential timeline, disharmonious frequencies would simply dissolve back to source, corresponding to the stable straight line represented in the graph. I would stand firmly in the conviction of my inner knowing, and on multiple occasions I shared and reinforced this optimal potentiality with my sister. Impressively, despite the obvious terror of this situation as a mother, she helped hold and strengthen this "high-vibe" outcome. This was a credit to her own fortitude, her baby's already impressive demonstration of her capacity to heal, and a tangible improvement in her blood work. Shortly before the dangerous biopsy, things took another very positive turn. A connection was discovered between the mass by her heart and an anomaly on her back. By grace, this allowed a very dangerous procedure to be avoided in favor of a less dangerous one. Of course, it was very serious and scary nonetheless, involving general anesthesia, the insertion of a PICC line to the heart for future delivery of medication, and a biopsy.

In late September, my niece had the procedure. As planned, my sister notified me that "She is going into the OR now." I instinctively replied, "So am I," not quite sure what that even meant. I lay down in the Wheel, heart open with love and gratitude. I figured I would connect with Spirit, pray, and channel love and light. After all, what else is there to do confronted with this situation. I felt my niece on my chest, connected at the heart, where we have been breathing together for months. In a single, mystical, breath I perceived an even more profound connection... she on her chest in the operating room, and me... as the table. From my perspective, I was somehow in the operating room with her in real time. The first twenty minutes were anxiety filled, and I had difficulty being still. I felt the dynamic emotions and the heart connection to my niece. My body thrashed around quite a bit where I lay, yet I also paradoxically felt the density and utter solidity of being a table. We breathed together and eventually found a peaceful repose. "It's Ok," I repeated assuredly, as I stroked her invisible head. Suddenly, she lovingly put her reply in my mind. "I know... I know what I'm doing!" The peace that accompanied that statement was palpably beautiful in my body.

During the initial agitated period in the OR, there arose a strong emotional field that was a cocktail of anxiety, fear, and suffering. I felt it deeply and all at once. Its source was not my niece, but rather the collective of people emotionally invested in the procedure. Such is the awesome power of attention in consciousness... that this subtle collective energy field had necessarily manifested around this story. As I was present multi-dimensionally, I was able to perceive and interact with this energy. Of course, this field of amassed "dark" emotions was present in the immeasurable expanse of the blissfield. Despite the ordeal, the beauty and love underlying it remained at the energetic forefront, continually revealing a deeper harmony within the totality of events. I projected love and light into the dark energy... through it's flowering, withering, and dying back to source. Only light remained. It was beautiful. I outstretched my arms as extensions of the table that I had embodied, and held the entire OR in the embrace of the Medicine Wheel, infusing it with healing light. My niece remained tightly anchored to my chest, moving perfectly with me as I rocked side to side on the floor. That sensation served to reinforce our unbreakable heart connection. There was a very real third-dimensional medical procedure going on, but also a very real mystical intervention.

Still holding the OR in the heart of the Wheel, I projected spheres of love and light at the doctors I envisioned on both sides of us, while continuously gently stroking my niece's head. Then, just as in our prior healing sessions together, Mother Mary filled the OR from above with showers of love, while Mother Earth graciously received the disharmonious frequencies from below. Shakti Panther, the beautiful white Wheel Spirit, then appeared on my chest, with my niece nestled between us. Her peaceful purr harmonized with the high vibratory energy of love and light that pervaded both the entire room and the unlimited expanse of the Medicine Wheel. Suddenly I felt a part of my niece's presence pull away, and a calm, peaceful sensation prevailed, complete with a sense of completion. Shakti Panther warmly communicated "We've got this from here." I opened my eyes. Joyous, grateful tears spilled out, and I lay in the blissfield, physically drained and blessed beyond measure.

To all of our great delight, the procedure went very well and the best possible diagnosis was rendered. It was not cancerous, after all. The mass was part of a network of vascular anomalies. It remained a very serious condition, but was treatable with oral medication. The intrusive PICC line, inserted in anticipation of a more dire diagnosis, was soon removed. It did not belong in the high vibratory outcome that we had been graced to collectively manifest. Over time, the anomalies should shrink and ultimately dissolve back to source.

So there you have it... part of my personal spiritual and energetic awakening story, and its unique expression in my life. Whenever I choose to end the written version, it will necessarily be "In medias res," in the middle of things, just as it began. For the "-ing" in awakening never goes away. The process is always unfolding as we are evolving, growing, loving, falling, rising, and just plain living. I refer to this tale as "an awakening story" in order to normalize it. It is not some unique event, but the natural trajectory of every human being. The individualized expression or particulars of any single human story will be vastly diverse. Yet, from a larger perspective, every human awakening story is the same: Consciousness, having seemingly separated itself from the singular totality of being by taking form, rediscovers its true nature in divine union with all life everywhere. Without exception, we are all somewhere in this story.

So take whatever resonates and leave the rest. You will get from it what you're supposed to, whatever that may be. Regardless of how real or fantastical you find these stories, they contain universal truths and lessons that are accessible despite any range of skepticism. This is so in the telling of any human story on any subject. No matter the circumstances, the Truth has an uncanny way of revealing itself at just the right moment. We are all awakening together, somewhere on the path. By some divine grace or power, the only being and consciousness that ever was will reveal itself within you... right on time. You will discover the true nature of your human potential and your essential divinity. It cannot be otherwise. Blessings and grace on your journey to becoming blissfully human, my brothers and sisters.

PART TWO
EMBODIMENT

The Mountain

WAIT A MINUTE... anyone reading the last few pages would assume the book had ended. They would be right. I had no more intention to type up Part Two than I did Part One. However, here we are. It is clear that I had caught up to the present day when I completed the first part. It was late 2019, just two years into the dramatic bio-spiritual awakening. I knew that the extraordinary unfolding was worth documenting for a number of potential reasons, but I didn't want to do the required work and had no interest in looking back while on this fast moving, expansive trajectory. My will was irrelevant. Titles, chapters, teachings, and full paragraphs started pouring out constantly on my walks. I battled with the idea of undertaking the project, with good reason, but it was evidently already being written. The Medicine Wheel made it clear that it was interested in the book, so I decided to get on board.

For two months I would do nothing but walk the beach and work on the book. Being an older fellow, I have never written anything of note that wasn't in pencil. This was no exception. I blistered my fingers and wrote it all out in several journals. It was like I was on autopilot, and I could do nothing else. Throughout the process I felt the assist of a divine hand... guiding me along with nurturing bliss, further elucidating the fantastical events, and providing language to help point to the indescribable. It was its own beautiful communion, and I am ever grateful for that blessing. Upon completion, I typed it up and printed a handful of copies. I must confess that the process of writing the book proved invaluable for this wayfarer, who had initially resisted the project. My awakening journey was unfolding rapidly, with barely a moment of respite between large, cosmic experiences. The time spent working on the book afforded me a great opportunity to reflect on the bigger picture and examine the nexus between various events. I would also more deeply metabolize the lessons and teachings as I relived the experiences. It was profoundly beneficial in that regard, as well as in helping to establish a firm foundation from which the journey would continue.

A final important point about the role of the book relates to a challenging issue for one undergoing such a transformation... disclosure. Speaking from my own experience, when Spirit awakens within you, it is nothing less than shock and awe to discover that you are not who you thought you were, at all. Not even close. Of course, that means that you are not who anyone else thinks you are, either. Thankfully, Spirit brings with her an innate intelligence and inner knowing to support and guide one through the process. Still, explaining it to someone else is another story altogether. How am I supposed to tell my loved ones about what is dominating my existence in a way that can be digested? It would take days to just fill someone in inadequately! Each piece really only makes sense in context with all the other pieces. A fragment of the story will not suffice.

Yet the attempt must be made, if only to a select few. The absence of such a sharing would remove the intimacy from my closest relationships, for I couldn't answer simple questions like "What's going on?" or "How are you?" with any authenticity. Awakening is already a journey one must necessarily walk alone, but a few supportive hearts on board go a long way. I sent a few friends and family a copy of the book as a sort of "coming out." That way, I thought, they could read the whole thing and then we could start our conversation from there, with some reference points if needed. This turned out to be an effective disclosure model and a blessing for me personally. Some very interesting and awkward conversations would obviously ensue, but the intimacy gap was quickly closed. I was able to fully "live my truth" within this tight circle, as my journey into the unknown progressed.

Anyway, here I am again, writing out the second half of the book. I have just finished living another year and a half of this story to a magical, mystical climax... and now it's pouring out. I still have no personal desire to write it into book form, but I was wise enough to journal most of the key happenings and stories in real time. Fortunately, I had learned the benefits of this practice and maintained it. I briefly resisted the more substantial project, but it was futile. It started writing itself again, so now I'm all in. We will pick up where we left off, and I will endeavor once more to share this unique expression of a universal transformation, as I perceived it.

It was the start of 2020... that alone will be the lead in countless dramatic and heartbreaking stories, for it marked the beginning of a global pandemic that would bring the world to a tenuous halt and claim a staggering number of souls. As it relates to this story, the pandemic did not generally alter the trajectory of the unfolding... nothing could. The Goddess would have her way. I had already been "social distancing" for two years since this wild journey began, so I wouldn't feel the impact of isolation like most people. I would continue my routine of grounding medicine walks, healing work, and spiritual study. I was already working minimally since the window surgery, just enough to survive while trying to navigate this extreme situation. With the societal shutdown, I was able to fully surrender to the process... every minute of every day. Though this scenario is not necessary for awakening, it was a blessing in my case. Things had been moving at a pace with which my body could barely keep up, and required my full attention. There was clearly more cosmic activity to come, and this way Spirit could just keep her foot on the gas. The shutdown did have one specific dramatic impact on this story... the beaches were temporarily closed. My crucial daily beach walks were suddenly illegal and abruptly halted! This place where I grounded and integrated vast energies, did healing work, and developed a sacred connection to Mother Earth, was now inaccessible. I must find a new path immediately. Allow me to introduce... the mountain.

My studio sits in a beautiful canyon that carves its way through the hills down to the ocean. Within a hundred yards of my door is a trail that ascends and descends a neighboring mountain in a narrow loop. At the top of the loop there is a lovely, grassy plateau with a beautiful view looking down the zigzagging valley to the coast. From there, a paved private road takes you the final leg to the top of the ridge. I affectionately call this Lizard Lane, home to many of my reptile friends. This provides the same spectacular view, only higher up, so it includes the grassy plateau in its vista. From both of these spots, you can also see a third point, which is about half way down the descending side of the loop. There is an interestingly carved four-foot boulder that sits at the edge of a clearing overlooking the same view, only lower. I call this Medicine Rock and always stop for a sit and a visit. When you turn around and look back up the mountain, you can see the previous two spots mentioned. The trinity of view sites is exquisitely aligned down the canyon toward the ocean, where I had spent the last two years walking. I would quickly make a daily routine of the mountain hike, stopping at each of the three points. Fortunately the trail was seldom used, so I rarely encountered any other humans. The mountain would be the primary setting and training ground for the next leg of the journey.

Before continuing with the narrative through which the transformation would further unfold, it is worth doing a reset as to the status of my multidimensional awakening. To do so, I will employ the ancient and oft used metaphor of the tree. Simply stated, the human being can be considered a tree with an infinite root system below that merges with the transcendent core of the Earth, and an infinite branch system above that merges with the transcendence of Source. In the present state of human consciousness, we largely only perceive the trunk. One may be aware of the roots and branches to various degrees, yet the transcendent is still rarely recognized in our daily, lived experiences. Using this cursory model, I would define a mystical experience as a dramatic encounter or connection to a transcendent root or branch. A common "root" example might produce a profound feeling of oneness with the Earth, nature, her creatures, or spirits. A common "branch" experience may be an astonishing divine synchronicity or a "third eye" vision of the typically unseen realms. Anyone reading this has likely had one or both. They are in fact available at all times, and it is the increasing recognition of this that often propels an awakening journey along.

Considering my particular case in light of the above tree paradigm, the events in Part One of this book could be described as going "full mystic." First, my physical and subtle bodies were radically transformed to handle the influx of vast energies associated with the expansion of consciousness. Once the vessel was prepared, Spirit awoke to herself within, in an incomprehensible divine explosion of the spiritual heart. The higher frequencies allowed for the transcendent connections at each pole of the "tree" to be realized and brought into the lived dimension of being. Basically, the full root and branch systems were irreversibly flipped on like a light switch, and the cyclical process of expansion and integration began. As my story continued to unfold, the prevailing theme would be the stabilization of these "Heaven and Earth" connections. There would be a merging of awakened consciousness into each of these two poles, bringing their transcendence into the phenomenal plane through embodied expression. Ultimately, all points would collapse into a seamless unity... leaving a harmonious divine singularity, absent any separation. The process would play out during medicine walks and healing sessions on the mountain. I will again endeavor to put words to the wordless.

The impact of the mountain on my connection with Mother Earth would be felt right away and strengthen exponentially. While the terrain was far more treacherous for the barefooted than the beach, it was doable, and for me, necessary. It required a slow, methodical pace, with great attention placed on the landing spot of every step. The soles of my feet were pretty tough at this point, but not impervious to the brambles, sticks and stones scattered across the trail. Diligently watching every step took my notion of walking meditation to the next level. One result was that I noticed every living creature in my path, from beetles to crickets to lizards to ant caravans... all moving with great intention. I became laser focused on not interfering with or ending the life of any of my Earth relations. It was a blossoming of the Eastern concept of "Ahimsa," commonly translated as "do no harm." While I most certainly fall well short of living this ideal to its full measure, this new practice on my walks produced immediate benefits. There was a profound recognition of my unity with all creatures, and I felt a deeper motherly embrace from the Earth herself, accompanied by beautiful waves of bliss. She was aware of this compassionate intention toward her children and lovingly made her appreciation known. During the weeks and months ahead, this would be evidenced by myriad synchronicities and communions with all species encountered on the trail. My Earth connection was also enhanced by the addition of walking on dirt rather than exclusively sand. Unlike the typical beach walk, there was a unique quality to every step. With a vast spectrum of soil textures, firmness, and even temperatures, each instance of contact revealed an exquisite individuality. Every step was absolutely full and complete, the whole world coming into being anew and dissolving on contact. My flesh joined with the flesh of the Earth, drawing us into a unity in which I am but a cell of her body. This is what I would come to consider "Walking in Beauty," or another might consider flowing with the course of the Dao. Joyous tears and ecstatic bliss were its dominant fragrance.

The mountain circuit provided an ideal structure in which to carry out the healing sessions of the Medicine Wheel. As soon as my bare feet hit the Earth, I would open a dialogue with the sacred Mother. "Hi Mother," I would always begin, and then like a Mantra I would alternate "thank you" and "I love you" with each step. Somehow, she would always respond to my presence... either by vibratory transmission or through an interaction with one of her creatures. Our deep connection established, we would walk in beauty together. For the remainder of the ascent, I invoked the Spirits of the Wheel and prepared the healing container. I would usually issue some sort of prayer at the top of the ridge, and then head back own. While descending, I brought forth the essence of each being with whom I was working, and allowed for the established healing practice to unfold or evolve into its next phase. This was usually complete by the time I made it down to Medicine Rock, where I did any critical additional work, before marinating in the healing love and light of the Wheel with all presences present. As further evidence of my precious Earth bond, Medicine Rock became an active member of the healing team, participating directly and ultimately "appearing" in the invisible Wheel. Thus the "root" system connection of the tree of my being would continue to grow in depth and luminosity.

Now let's turn to the other pole of the transcendent vertical column, the "branch" system or cosmic component. My connection to this divine aspect climaxed with the remarkable communion with Jesus in which I was graced with a direct experience of the Cross. Jesus would now work on stabilizing this connection, through a particular Wheel healing taking place on the mountain over the next few months. The specific details of the healing are personal in nature and not mine to share, but the manner in which Jesus was involved and working on my process, is relevant to my awakening journey. Ok, all of this divine union and Jesus talk is going to require another brief expository digression before we move ahead. How is it that I speak of a divine union at one moment and then of a relationship between separate beings in the next? Which is it? Well, depending on the perceptual lens or lenses through which your awareness is focused, both can be true... a quintessential spiritual paradox.

I'd like to introduce the ancient concept of the "Ishta Deveta" to help with this seeming contradiction. The commonly used translation of the Sanskrit is "cherished divinity," as in a personal God, or that divine expression or personification that is most resonant with your individual conditioning. Let us consider creation and manifestation as a vast expanding movement in consciousness, from a singular unity of impersonal pure being to the vast multiplicity and density of planet Earth. All along the way, there are myriad levels and spectra of energy teeming with life. At higher frequencies and dimensions, Ascended Masters, Angels, and the like, can be viewed as archetypal energies or expressions of that singular divine Source. When consciousness in a human being awakens to these planes, those universal energies can be actualized... embodied with a particular vibratory signature or identity, and related to as a personal aspect of divinity. When the spiritual adept awakens to the shocking revelation of the infinite, the appropriate "Ishta Deveta" is there to guide the emerging soul through the strata of seemingly separate consciousness. By Grace, the individual aspirant and the particularized deity merge into ecstatic union, and then ultimately into the impersonal singularity from which our creation originally sprang. This is the basic understanding of the concept, and I offer it as reflective of my own experience.

Although I practiced no form of religion or worship prior to my spontaneous awakening, based on my cultural upbringing and life experience, it is logical that Jesus would serve in this role for my personal journey. In our initial mystical encounter, he purposefully didn't "appear," so as not to reinforce our separateness and add an unnecessarily delay to the realization of our union. I was truly blessed that our connection began from this most intimate space in the infinite depths of my heart... closer than close... closer than the breath itself. Because of this, I am acutely aware of the profound Grace at play in my particular story. In my rather extensive spiritual studies to discover the nature of what was happening to me, I read the writings of many Saints and mystics from throughout the ages. It provided an invaluable understanding of some of the stages and processes of awakening, and it helped me learn and formulate different ways to language the transformation. I read a number of the Christian mystics, with whom I resonated greatly. To name a few, it was in the direct experiences of St. Teresa of Avila, St. John of the Cross, St. Symeon, and St. Catherine of Sienna, that I found expressions and mystical encounters that most closely mirrored my own. Apparently, I too am a "Cross" devotee, and that sacred Tree would be the template or structure through which my journey would continue to unfold.

During a series of mountain healing sessions on behalf of a powerfully radiant being, Jesus took the lead with me in her service, while simultaneously leading me into our inevitable union. It is the latter movement that is relevant to my transformation story. This healing was already notably different than prior ones in a number of ways. In the first place, Jesus stepped forth in the Wheel immediately to guide the healing. Also, the Wheel activity normally has a directed energetic component, like a transmission or purge, typically involving a particular motion and a specific intention. This time the healing was exclusively verbal. A "higher" aspect or essence of my "transitioning" sister sat upon Medicine Rock in the multi-dimensional space. I stood directly in front of her and spoke her medicine spontaneously from the depths of my being. The Wheel portal served to bring the words through to her at the soul level, which could then be introduced to her individualized presence... to inform her form, so to speak. The other notable difference in this healing is that the main theme or focus of the talks was at the soul level. What I mean is that rather than the substance of the session being about how an event or situation harmonizes in this life, it was about how this lifetime harmonizes into the larger soul story of many lifetimes. The medicine talks were both beautiful and profound, and it was in this context and sacred space that Jesus would move with earnestness to reel me in.

A number of mystical movements and events would happen in fairly rapid succession, all serving to further dissolve the apparent division between my "Ishta Deveta" and myself. I'll describe a few. The first movement was a sudden shift in my Wheel position. Since its current iteration, I have been positioned in the West, facing Jesus in the East position of source energy. One day I called forth the Wheel energy as usual, and it immediately spun 180 degrees to orient me in the East. It was final and absolute. Any manifestation of me in another position produced an immediate rotational effect returning me to the East. We are one, Jesus communicated, of the same divine light. There is no position in which we are not both present. I quickly acknowledged this and have been operating in the East ever since.

The next phenomenon I would describe as a dance in consciousness, expanding and contracting through levels of perception, like breathing. I would be expressing a medicine talk from the depths of my being, and then Jesus would take over mid flow. There was a clear perceptual shift from speaking from the soul level to being "instrumentalized" by another. Then the breath of consciousness would further expand until our soul level division was absent, and from a divine singularity I spoke as both Jesus and myself simultaneously... with no distinction. There would be several such mystical "breaths" during these sessions. In retrospect, it was vital spiritual training to have my consciousness flex in this way while I was rooted on the Earth walking about in broad daylight.

After just a few days of this cosmic dance ensuing, my beloved Master would add another layer of to the unity mix, before a final punctuation mark. Several of the medicine talks referenced the cloak of Jesus, a symbolic reference to the power of Faith found in scripture. In faith an aspirant had touched His cloak, and by the power and purity of her faith, she was instantly healed... and Jesus said as much. After each healing session concluded, I would dismount Medicine Rock and float down the rest of the trail in pure bliss and peace, usually weeping tears of uncontainable beauty. It is hard to imagine or convey how this is perceived purely energetically, but one magical day Jesus covered me with his cloak for the final leg of the trail home, emphasizing that we were one... I was He... He was I. I was the very cloak itself, he added, embodied and available to be touched in Faith and facilitate healing in that same, full measure. That may already be difficult enough to accept, but the mystical pedal was to the metal and Jesus would soon punctuate his unity argument.

The Wheel was in full bloom as I made my descent towards Medicine Rock, delivering a fresh dose of verbal medicine, when Jesus took over once again. He shared a beautiful message about events and eras of great darkness, in which there is also necessarily great light... and therefore great opportunity. Death and birth are always together, and we are well served to turn our focus to the rebirth that death offers. It was a glorious sermon. I outstretched my arms in front of me in gratitude, saying "Thank you, Jesus!" As I spoke his name I beheld a fresh, bleeding puncture wound in the center of my left palm. I was astounded. To the best of my memory, I hadn't touched a single thing on this walk and certainly didn't feel the wound being made. I assumed I would have noticed that, as the pain of the puncture was very real and present immediately upon discovery. In fact, it kept me up that night and hurt for three days. Of course, I thought that perhaps I touched a tree at the beginning of the walk and was too cosmically distracted to notice... and then the pain was psychosomatically instigated on sight. Yet that still meant that a minimum of an hour had passed, and the wound appeared brand new. I also might have seen it already, considering the way I wave my hands and arms around while I am engaged in the Medicine Wheel. I went home in a stunned, blissful state.

A few hours later, I settled down and sat in reflection on the divine synchronicity, regardless of how it really happened. I had rolled through Holy week and thought that my uncanny stigmata streak had come to an end, but perhaps not. I facetiously spoke aloud to Jesus, "You're slipping, Brother... You missed Holy week by a month and a hand puncture is a repeat, anyway!" He responded immediately with a perceivable cosmic smile, communicating that it was the other hand this time! Also that the timing was on me... he was just responding to the sincerity of my thank you in a way that furthered our union. It was his way of saying, "We are one... You're doing it... you are the Christ speaking." I marveled at how after all of the miraculous events and spectacular encounters on my journey, some part of me still wanted to rationalize the events and explain it away. "I must still have a trace of 'Doubting Thomas' in me," I said aloud resignedly. "Look at the hole right now," Jesus insisted, "I just gave you a hole."

The mountain was proving to be a most transformational setting, and though location is not ultimately determinative on the journey, interacting with nature in solitude full-time was extremely powerful. Over several months, my Ishta Deveta was reeling me into the transcendent branch system and Mother Earth was drawing my root system into her infinite core. I was having frequent and deepening connections with the Earth herself, and miraculous interactions with her various creatures as a part of that communion. I'll share one exquisite, relevant example. It was now early May 2020, and I had just ascended to the top of the ridge on my medicine walk. The Wheel was fully engaged, the presence of the Spirit team was palpable, and I stopped at the top to take in the view for a few minutes. I spied a lone Eagle across the canyon about a quarter mile, which I quickly associated with the hovering Eagle in Sedona that marked the upward position of the Wheel. I stood and watched her fly across the canyon directly at me, gradually dropping in elevation to match mine on the way. The Eagle arrived with a great swoosh, such that I could feel the wind displaced by the magnificent bird. She came within six feet of my head and her wingspan was nearly as big as mine. I could see incredible detail, particularly the great muscles of her wings as she flew directly beneath the sun, which acted like an x-ray machine. And there was a sublime profound eye contact that I had never before experienced with a bird.

After the initial fly-by, the Eagle immediately returned and started flying slow, methodical, tight circles just above my head. Spontaneously I began chanting and spinning with my wings spread wide to match the great bird while it circled. Powerful Shakti energy gushed through my body and radiated spherically outward to encompass my feathered friend. Incredibly, we danced together this way for over a minute. She varied the diameter between ten and twenty feet, but kept me as the center of our cosmic funnel. I rotated with gliding outstretched arms, mimicking her graceful, banking motion. We were intimately aware of each other, and my entire being was blissfully luminous. Joyful tears flowed freely onto the flesh of the Earth. Then she suddenly banked and dipped out of sight, so I began my soaring descent, wings still stretched wide. Seconds later she reappeared from below the ridge, again passing just feet from my head. She resumed circling me while I soared down Lizard Lane. We were moving swiftly, but she stayed positioned above me. I followed her lead with my arms, and so we danced. I even took the lead to see what would happen... I broke rhythm, slowed dramatically, and reversed the direction of my banking motion. She noticed, circled back, and locked into the new pattern that I had created. We danced for another hundred yards before a second Eagle appeared and drew her away. It was a profound communion and blessing, and the power, love, and light thus generated was beautifully brought to bear in the healing Wheel session that ensued.

The increasing connectivity and stabilization of the energetic anatomy's "root" and "branch" systems were heading somewhere with intention... to a mystical union in which the two transcendent poles would collapse into a singularity in the infinite depths of the omnipresent spiritual heart. I will attempt to convey how this completely radical, yet natural and universal awakening process was expressed and perceived in my particular story. I told a dear friend, who had the ears and heart to hear such a tale, about dancing with Eagle on the mountain. In response, she gifted me an eagle feather that she had on her altar for over a decade. Hearing my story, she felt an inner knowing that it was supposed to go to me, so she decided to "dress" and send it. She had a well-formulated idea of how she would adorn it, but the feather intervened and directed her otherwise. She complied with the wishes of the feather. It arrived at my door in late May. I could feel the vibrant energy of the feather before I opened the box. When I revealed it, I felt its power even more strongly. Our energy fields comingled in this physical meeting, but it felt more like a reunion than an introduction. It was a blissful encounter indeed. I found her a nice home in the g-bubble, and placed her lovingly as I expressed my gratitude for her presence. She was received and welcomed by the full expanse of the Wheel. That night, as I got ready for bed, I invited her to share her beautiful, unique medicine at any time. The following ensued...

The current was high, within and without, and again I had the undeniable feeling that my empty room was crowded. I could only meet the moment. I stepped into the center of the g-bubble and engaged the Spirits. The Wheel presented in full bloom and I began a spontaneous healing session. I went around to each essence present, praying and healing as normal, but with one unique difference... a particular felt sensation and knowing that I was everyone in the Wheel. For example, instead of saying "A" has cancer and "B" has trauma, I said, "I have cancer" and "I have trauma," etc. As I went through the various diagnoses, I could see clearly how conditions and patterns in my own life corresponded with each one... the "cancer" or "trauma" in my own life. Aside from all the beautiful individual interactions and healings that take place in the Wheel, there was a renewed recognition that I am the universal patient.

When I finished the round, I found myself facing the position of Mary Magdalene, whom I addressed with devotional reverence. I expressed a deep gratitude for the various loves and relationships I had been gifted to learn and grow from. This was not out of the blue, but the subject of some of the healing work on myself revealed in the current Wheel session. I communicated that despite the heartbreaks and resulting wounds, I was both fine and appreciative. I may have messed up on the "soul mate" thing, I confessed, but I know for certain that it is all as it should be. Then, without forethought, I turned to Jesus' neighboring spot in the Wheel and added, "Though you know how much I still love her." I was surprised by my own words for an instant, but then my entire being was filled with an unspeakable peace and nurturing love. Every photon of angst present in my being was incinerated in the fire of its radiance. The benediction gloriously filled the entire space and I stood frozen in the rapture, staring straight ahead at my invisible Ishta Deveta. And then the miraculous would unfold.

Before my very eyes... my two earthly eyes... a golden hued silhouette manifested in the room right in front of me. It's aura intensified and brightened until a clearly defined, yet transparent light body stood before me. It was just arms length away and appeared to be about seven feet tall. There were no distinct features at all within the outline of the subtle form. But there was no doubt as to who it was... for, once perceived, the vibratory signature of Jesus is unmistakable and impervious to imitation or deception. I stood in absolute awe as fountains of bliss flowed through me, and fountains of tears flowed out. I reached out my arms, placed my hands above the crown of the Angelic head, and slowly traced down and up the contour of the mesmerizing form. After a few minutes, the luminous figure moved slowly, but surely towards me. I remained frozen in place, yet fearless, while the radiant essence superimposed itself on me and we became one. Time for another issuance of our now familiar refrain, as the ecstasy and profundity of that union is entirely unapproachable with words! As we merged, a wave passed through my body and flushed, cleansed, and purged my entire being. I could feel the purifying effect viscerally, and I was overcome with peace, joy, and love. My body began to tremble in the overwhelming field of bliss.

I became so wobbly that my knees buckled and I pleaded with Mother Earth to root me in solidly, so I could remain still in this phenomenal space and energy. She complied immediately. It was like gravity had been instantly increased a thousand fold and I was made the trunk of an elder Redwood, locked on her surface with an enduring stability. A moment later I felt my roots extend down to her very core. I stood firmly in the center of the Earth and her surface at the same time, abuzz with the blissful vastness that was every bit as present within and without my body... all borders had vanished. The light body before me was gone, but the space still shone with its essence. That's when I realized that the light was coming from my own being. I was lighting up the room, and Love was pouring into, through, and out of my heart. Still weeping continuously, I stared straight ahead and the light show would continue. The invisible "emptiness" in the room became visible. I could clearly see the wall of my studio ahead, yet somehow I could also see the space that I was looking through. It was nebulous, wispy, and whimsical, yet with a perceivable organization underlying it. I sensed the limitless expanse of my vision and the visible emptiness became the sky... and then deep space... and then vast universe all at once.

I think it safe to say that I am utilizing three eyes at this point. I felt like a cosmic eagle. I kept seeing shooting stars in my periphery, as well misty clouds and lots of celestial bodies and light formations... and still my wall! I remained in this position and vision for about forty unbelievable minutes, anchored in the center of the Earth and the center of the Cosmos. During this miraculous span, I outstretched my arms again and starting tracing where the now gone torso of the light body had been. Most spectacularly, as I did so, the heads of animals began appearing in the contoured space. They consisted of that same golden aura color, only this time with enough interior detail to discern the different animal faces. Each one stayed for about a minute. Tiger was first. I don't have full recall as to every animal and their order, but they included Bear, Lion, and Elephant, who extended his energetic trunk and "pet" me! Tiger was also the last to appear... the Alpha and Omega of the animal visions. Finally, completely exhausted, my highly energized body collapsed on the couch and settled into a welcome relaxed state. It was one of the better nights sleep I've had since this whole "awakening" began.

The next morning I awoke refreshed, vital, and energetically stable. I headed for the mountain for the first time since sacred eagle feather had come into my possession. I hoped I would see my eagle friend at the summit again, and extended the mystical invitation. The manifest world seemed a photon lighter on this morning, and I felt a deep Earth connection from the very first step. Our reunion was magical. Only half way up the trail, two eagles banked up from below and passed startlingly close to my head, such that I flinched dramatically. They began flying a tight circle about ten feet over my head. As before, there was a mutual awareness, and I began to dance in place with them... arms wide, spinning, banking, and chanting in the centerless center. The Wheel and its energy were noticeably empowered by this movement, and two more eagles arrived and joined the vortex, circling a little wider and about 40 feet above the first two. After multiple magnificent rotations, a third pair magically arrived and added a third concentric circle to the vortex, about five hundred feet high! The funnel shape was clearly defined and my body began trembling with the energy and its corresponding bliss. For a glorious minute I danced in the eye of the luminous Wheel with six eagles. Then all six birds flew away together towards the top of Lizard Lane. I hoped that they would meet me there, but they did not. In fact, I have yet to see an eagle since that exquisite morning dance.

Sacred Mother Earth and I would play the bird dance game together many times. I have danced with hawks, crows, turkey vultures, and more... from a single bird to more than a dozen. I recall feeling somewhat self-conscious about flapping around on the mountain, especially at the beginning of the dance craze, but given the circumstances the only real choice was to dance. At least no one saw, or so I thought. As it happened, nearly a year later on an adjacent part of the trail that I rarely walk, a woman approaching me on a mountain bike stopped dead in her tracks. She had a look of wonder on her face and said essentially the following: You're the guy... I saw you last year on the mountain when I was riding along the top of the ridge. There wasn't a bird in the sky until you arrived, and then suddenly a whole bunch appeared from every direction and started circling your head while you were spinning. It was absolutely amazing! When you left, all the birds flew away and again there wasn't a bird in the sky. I don't know what you were channeling, but it was definitely working. I acknowledged that it was I, stepped aside so she could pass, and she rode away without further inquiry. There was a beautiful welling up of Spirit as I recognized and acknowledged that She was doing all kinds of work that I wasn't aware of. Beholding that scene had been an instigating spark on the mountain biker's awakening journey, and I felt profoundly blessed to have played a role in her divine play.

And so it went on the mountain through the spring of 2020, full of mysteries and wonders beyond comprehension. The infinite "root" and "branch" systems of my tree being had been stably connected and enlivened during this powerful phase of the transformation. An all encompassing love affair with Mother Earth had ignited and drawn me into the unity of her infinite embrace... as a cell of her great body, as another bird in her sky, and as her very being, the totality of which

I also paradoxically contain within me. And my beloved Ishta Deveta, Jesus, who met me at the gateless gate of infinity, would take my hand and guide me through to the knowledge that I was He all along. He intentionally hadn't "appeared" to me in any way, to avoid suggesting that we were separate... with one blessed exception. And when he did finally momentarily manifest a light body, it was only to merge with me and concretize our sacred union. Summer approached and the beaches were reopened for walking. I worked it back into my medicine walk rotation, but continued to do the mountain at least four times a week. On many days, I did both.

The Blood

I WAS STILL flying high from my recent breakthrough and magical experience of unity consciousness. While it is clear at this point that the awakening process is unending, I sensed that I had hit a notable milestone. Something of that transcendent night would remain with me forever. My consciousness had realized a new level or dimension that it could now include while expanding and contracting as it breathed through life. As to my individual status, I felt a renewed sense of sovereignty and resolution to authentically live the Truth. The baseline vibration and intensity of energy in my body were higher than ever, but stable. I was globally invigorated, all my senses felt keenly receptive, and I enjoyed a heightened sharpness and clarity of mind. I was deeply rooted in the body and Earth, yet simultaneously often felt like I barely touched the ground. My medicine walks and healing sessions were both profound and powerful. While being utilized to help others, I received my own beautiful teachings and lessons to learn. I was extremely grateful and blessed to be a servant of Love in God's cosmic play. We are all really just radiant balls of divine light, and by Grace, I actually felt like one.

The summer of 2020 would come in with a mystical bang, on the evening of the Solstice. You may be familiar with the oft-cited phrase, "Where there is great light, there is great darkness." This is the case at any level of polarity consciousness, and I would experience that truth in a new multidimensional way. Apparently, the increasing radiance of my little ball of light had become intense enough to draw some attention. I was already familiar with this potentiality, as it had happened earlier on my journey after a perceived jump in luminosity. I haven't mentioned this subject yet, so I'll flashback a year for a brief recounting of a relevant story. Leaving the metaphysics aside, this is what happened. I lay on the beach with no one around, reveling in my newfound bliss, when suddenly a man sat nearby on a rock to one side of me... a little odd, but no big deal and no weird vibe. Then I felt an eerie dark presence to my other side. I saw nothing, but didn't doubt its existence as the powerful, intimidating wave washed through my field.

In a flash, I perceived the energy move into the man, who was now projecting the powerful darkness. He had previously paid me no mind, but was now staring me down as if he wanted to make eye contact, which we did. My "feeling" of being watched was now blatantly evident. I instinctively knew that I was being tested... How fearless was I? How powerful? Could I stand in that power? I definitely wasn't afraid and I knew that I could handle the situation. I lay back down confidently, closed my eyes, and "fired up" my field. My luminous protective sphere was impenetrable, and grew in intensity until only it could be perceived. The dark energy was overwhelmed, like a candle next to the sun. After a few moments, sensing only beauty, I opened my eyes and the man was casually strolling toward the water. He was energetically restored and the dark presence was absent. I was largely encouraged by this episode, as it indicated a continued expansion of my perception, and I felt like I had acquitted myself well. I passed the test by some measure, but by another measure I had failed. I would understand how during my next encounter with the "dark side".

That brings us back to Solstice 2020... It was late at night and I was feeling too vibrant to sleep, so I stepped outside my door for a little stargazing. I do this often, and have even come up with my own constellations and names. I would have only a minute to play with the stars, as my awareness would be quickly jolted away. I sensed a "dark" energy again... to my left about fifteen feet away. I thought I could make out a misty dark gray cloud about my size, but it was dark out and only a trace of light from the neighbor's lamppost illumined the scene. This time when the dark energy moved through me it made the beach incident feel like child's play. I felt no fear, though I was startled by it's power. Apparently, my transcendental union with the Divine produced such radiance that it merited attention again, and a "great light" would have to be met with a "great darkness." Not only did I feel like I was being checked out, but I perceived an intentional enmity, like it had a personality and didn't like me!

Fortunately, I was absolutely secure in the knowledge that I was invulnerable to any dark intentions. The Christ light or divine energy that my form had been transformed to embody is untouchable. There was no thought process as to what I should do, but rather the action flowed spontaneously. I gazed into the darkness... "Well, hello there," I said warmly, "Welcome." In response, the dark presence exploded in stature and power. I was now able to perceive it multi-dimensionally, and it blackened as it swelled to about twelve to fourteen feet high. The ensuing wave of energy intensified exponentially and swept through every cell of my body. It was indescribable, but if I had to pick a word, it would be "Evil." Now in the previous brush with darkness, I had acted to protect myself. I was blessed to be more than adequately empowered to do so, and it was a simple affair. But everything was different now. I was different now, and further along the path. My instinct wasn't to protect myself from darkness, but rather to heal it... to love it to death. For the open heart that truly loves has nothing to protect. I invite you to read that last sentence again.

I held my gaze, my stance, and my open heart. I felt the massive dark power, but was undisturbed. My being was aflame with light, as a torrent of divine current had arisen within to meet the moment. There was a sublime element of awe as I beheld the two great energetic polarities coexisting right next to each other. Bathed in light, I affectionately repeated my welcome and asked how I may help the impressively dark being. A powerful feeling of empathy arose in my heart, and I was overwhelmed with compassion for the entity and his dark prison. "You're gonna need a lot of Love," I told my brother, "You need to be loved... But you have come to the right place and you can have as much as you need." That said, I turned around and went back inside. Mysteriously, as I stepped in, I found myself in the middle of a healing session. As If picking up where I left off, I began speaking directly to the now unseen presence before me. I was administering the very Love medicine that I had just prescribed outside. The embodied sensation of this transformational energy was magnificently vibrant, and its purity and incorruptibility undeniable. After less than five minutes, the negative energy had dissipated and I no longer felt the presence of the entity.

I sat for a few minutes in stunned silence while my awareness contracted and settled back into my body. "Good Lord, Brother!" I said to Jesus when I realized what had just occurred. "I'm just a baby in all of this, and here I am acting like I can take on the darkest of the dark!" "You did," He communicated, "You can... and anyway, I am always with you." I marinated in the palpable bliss produced by that response, and thought to myself, I wonder who that being was? Jesus answered my query with an image in my mind's eye that lasted for a fraction of a second. It was specific being, still unknown to me, with clear distinct features that revealed a vicious looking demon. I was at such a level of luminosity on the journey that I had attracted the attention of a particularly heavy-duty, dark being. All wild mysticism aside, it is worth repeating that the real value of this story lies in the following universal Truth: In the face of darkness, the healing act is not to protect oneself from it, but rather to cast light upon it... and the ultimate light is Love. Thereby, darkness can be transmuted and integrated back into the light, rather than left in tact.

For the rest of the summer and into the fall, the unfolding continued in a relatively routine manner. Every day I walked in beauty barefoot on the Earth, either on the beach, the mountain, or both. I engaged and facilitated healing sessions in the Medicine Wheel and operated through the sustained and strengthening connections of my total "treeness." I lovingly communed with the Sacred Mother that held me, the Divine Mother that filled me, and the Christ that lived me into the World. That turned into it's own little walking mantra...

"Held, Filled, Lived". As I had been for some time, I was basically in a constant meditative state of contemplative prayer, gratitude, and devotion. My sleeping patterns were still rather erratic, but not a problem, and I was otherwise basically symptom free. The "enlightening" of the subtle energetic body continued to progress, and there were regular multi-day spans where I could clearly feel heightened current and vibratory adjustments. It was a most beautiful time in a most blessed life. I knew everything on every level of existence to be a divine expression emerging from the infinite ground of being. This is how I walked around... then and now. The bliss was there. The tears were there.

Another noteworthy development was the growing number of teachings, lessons, and medicine talks pouring out of me... fully vocalized, as if more than just my invisible tribe was present. It felt like teacher training for an inevitable time when I would be sharing my story, and helping to guide or orient others on theirs. I was also receiving some specific healing "suggestions" from Jesus when relevant. Most prominently is the frequent refrain, "Don't be afraid to use your hands!" He clearly means this to apply to both Wheel sessions and interactions with people in daily life. In his most recent iteration he interjected, "Don't forget about our healing hands... don't hesitate to lay our hands... I just may use them, as I always have." We both knew that there had been moments where I could have done so and did not. I have struggled on the journey with that self-conscious element that caused me to shrink in those moments. I have largely self-corrected, yet know that I shall surely revisit this issue during my ongoing refinement.

The other main healing "tip" from Jesus has to do with the eyes, and their laser-like power to direct "Shakti" or divine energy, just like the hands. There were even a number of "visions" that accompanied this teaching, exhibiting various scenarios of me healing with the eyes. The locking of eyes is one primary usage, relevant to either physical or psychological trauma. In this there is the ability to connect deeply at the heart level, through the proverbial "windows of the

115

soul", and therefore bypass the tortured mind and exigent circumstances unfolding at the story level of experience. In the case of acute physical trauma, it can take the edge off of real physical pain. As for emotional or mental trauma, it offers a peaceful repose, even if short-lived. I can confirm this to be true from my own experience.

The next key inflection point on my awakening journey is best characterized by a cluster of profound states of consciousness that would occur in the fall of 2020. So far, I have described a variety of "mystical" experiences and bliss states, wherein consciousness has expanded to perceive a greater range of its multi-dimensionality. There has been a progression of sorts... greater levels of Shakti brought further expansion, which led to heightened perception, that produced more Shakti... and around and around we go. The most recent merging into a unity consciousness opened a perceptual door to a vast new cosmic frontier to be revealed, explored, and integrated. The next set of stories feature experiences that do just that. More frequent and prolonged immersions in high vibratory states would serve to both stabilize the recent expansion, and continue preparing the vehicle for service.

Having employed the phrase unity consciousness, I realize I am referencing a term with established parameters and connotations. I would like to be clear that I am speaking only from personal experience. When I say unity, it is not to locate myself on a known spectrum or chart, but because that is the best word to describe my lived experience. However, before returning to the narrative, I'd like to briefly frame the general issue of "transcendental consciousness." The simplest definition is commonly held to be anything other than our normal three cycling states of waking, dreaming, and deep sleep. The Sanskrit term is "Turiya," which literally means the "fourth." This transcendental fourth state has been further divided and subdivided into various levels, which include some familiar spiritual terms like cosmic, God, and unity consciousnesses. These terms are certainly useful as guideposts or for orientation purposes, but it would be inaccurate to consider them as steps on a formulaic path. This suggests a rigid linearity, rather than the fluid undulating nature of expansion and contraction in my experience. The stories shall tell the story, so to speak... as consciousness breathed in and out, through the different dimensions and perceptual lenses.

Finally, it is both relevant and helpful to introduce another spiritual term and Sanskrit favorite, "Samadhi." It's another word with many shades of meanings, levels, and applications, but I will employ it in a rather general way. As simply defined by Paramahansa Yogananda in his famous autobiography, it is "a state of God consciousness." By this basic definition, you can see how samadhi is a naturally occurring, constant state for the Yogi... for an element of God union, once realized, always remains. I know this ever-present remnant intimately from my own experience. So we will consider this as our natural, blissful baseline state. When I speak of "going into" samadhi moving forward, I am referring to a dramatic, episodic surge of divine current and connectivity, with vibrant bliss coursing through every cell of the body and beyond. That's what I mean... a powerful eruption of bliss from within the natural bliss. I will avoid the various Sanskrit modifiers enumerated in the different traditions. Again, the stories must tell the story. I certainly can't discuss a "flavor" of samadhi that I haven't directly tasted... like one that is fully detached from physical sensation, or one that doesn't feature profound bliss. After all, my awakening story began in earnest with an explosion of vibratory bliss in the heart. Shakti flooded my total being as divine current and has remained ever since. Now, back to the narrative...

It is mid October, following a relatively smooth span of stabilization and integration. Walking in beauty on the sacred Earth and offering healing sessions in the Wheel remained a daily affair. One Friday afternoon on the mountain, I had completed the activity of the Wheel session as I approached Medicine Rock on my descent. The current was high and my being was pervaded by bliss and beauty. I perched upon my rock friend and beheld the glorious canyon, winding down to the sacred stretch of ocean where such wondrous blessings had been gifted me. Ok... time for our fun new signifier... after a few moments,

I went into a powerful, ecstatic state of samadhi! The energetic flow was astounding, like a finely tuned engine purring effortlessly in its maximum revved position. Despite the ferocity of the Shakti, I felt entirely stable. I was simultaneously fully rooted in my physicality, and in harmonious resonance with the divine vibrations presenting in the subtler realms. There was an instant recognition of a sublime balance in consciousness. The lenses of perception were clear, open, accessible, connected, and engaged. Yet awareness did not favor any one in particular, and from this choice-less state of equanimity, was free to stretch its attention toward any lens without retracting itself from all the others. I was experiencing my multi-dimensional being with an expanded coherence and clarity, and though alone, it was happening out in the world.

From this borderless state of non-directed presence arose a spectacular movement in divine union. I was fully present as myself, as merged with Jesus, and as the universal Consciousness that informs and empowers both individual expressions. And what's more, all of that is birthed and emerging from the infinite core of the spiritual heart within. So now what the heck do I mean when I say "I"? I usually mean what everybody else means... but not always. This arising pronoun ambiguity reflects the paradoxical challenge of using a dualistic language to express a non-dual reality. In brief, somehow the obvious pronoun that would normally be deemed correct, simply no longer feels appropriate or accurate. I've even created my own linguistic band-aid to prevent from stumbling in conversation or adding too many qualifiers. I have added the plural "I" and the singular "we" to my personal vocabulary, so I could make sense and still feel internally authentic and accurate in expression! The singular "I" who likes peanut butter ice cream is profoundly different from the plural "I" who facilitates a healing in the Medicine Wheel. I'll leave it for you to decide which "I" sits atop Medicine Rock.

I began to spontaneously orate scriptural teachings, as if I was delivering a sermon to the entire coastline. Suddenly, I had a wild mystical vision. The broader symbolic meaning would become more clear days later in the unfolding events of our next story, but for now I will simply describe the experience as perceived in the moment. In blissful samadhi, I sat as "one" with my stone friend, who now presented as the Rock of Truth... so, I was now the Rock of Truth. We mystically expanded in unison into a massive boulder taller than the surrounding mountains, and then thundered down the zigzagged valley like a bowling ball, pulverizing everything in its worldly path. All that was not the truth was crushed into a powder that disintegrated in our powerful wake, leaving only the Real... absent of illusion.

"We" crashed into the receptive ocean eagerly awaiting our arrival, thereby establishing a sacred link uniting the mountain, the beach, and the Earth that connects them. I was also aware that I was Christ upon an ethereal stone chariot, and more perplexingly, a Dolphin Christ. The understanding was that, having left the singular dolphin consciousness to carry out a worldly service mission, "I" was now returning to the pod as part of the collective. While this particular thread of the story is strange and may make little sense, that's what happened... and the celebratory reunion was vibrant and magical indeed! The overwhelming joy expressed by the dolphins flooded the totality, and tears and bliss abounded.

On the following Monday, I would return to the beach for the first time since the Rock of Truth vision, and its context and import would be further elucidated. I soaked in the sun and read a few pages from the writings of St. Catherine, before pausing to gaze at the glimmering sea. In sat in open-eyed stillness and found myself in a vibrant state of samadhi in less than a minute. I invoked the Medicine Wheel and it presented in full bloom instantly. In perceiving the dolphin presence that always encircles the Wheel, the dramatic reunion from the Rock of Truth vision flashed in my awareness. I began to speak... "Honey, I'm home," I proclaimed to the dolphins! I sensed a wordless acknowledgement and an all-encompassing peaceful wave of "completion" washed through me. Mysteriously, I did in fact feel like a welcome home. "We are together again," I continued, "Here and now... I'll swim with you out there, and you sit with me here on the beach."

Somehow the state of samadhi would find another gear. When one wouldn't think it possible, measureless bliss erupted from within, and the visible world took on a most magical, luminous quality. Beheld through my teary eyes, while my body literally trembled from the vast flow of current, the world appeared with a pristine beauty and purity... revealing all manifestation as an expression of divinity.

Merged with the Dolphin collective and perceiving through that lens, there came the recognition that this is how dolphins always see the world. There is an astounding reconciliation of the relative and absolute realms, and the same indescribable beauty and divine presence pervades all lenses of awareness. We sat in profound union, merged and immersed. There was simply a man sitting alone on the beach, and yet this fulsome, invisible multi-dimensional scene was simultaneously playing out. I was in the world, but not of it. I remained in ecstatic silence, marveling at the manner in which the sun's exquisite radiance produced such incomparable beauty. I reached out with intention toward the sun with my "laser" eyes and my individual field exploded with light. I both witnessed and lived the presence of a second sun within this very form, shooting sacred divine light outward through all openings, including the standard stigmata wounds and the mouth. My breath resembled a dragon breathing the primordial fire of creation and destruction. There were two suns... one in the heavens and one in the spiritual heart, their radiances colliding and merging in the manifest world... and yet it was the same light, and the same sun. As sure as I was sitting there in the body, I was in everything else and everything else was in me... the dolphins, the suns, the ocean, the Earth, the light, the totality.

Interestingly, during this most wondrous union, I never saw an actual dolphin in the water. There were, however, a plethora of birds! I had set up near a fairly large group collected on the beach, and was enjoying the company of my feathered friends. Most notably, there were also several dozen birds about a hundred yards out to sea directly in front of me, bobbing up and down on the sunlit water. I had noticed the cluster upon arrival, and they had remained floating in stillness throughout. Now as I looked out through the multi-dimensional sunlight, I saw that the birds had gathered closer together, and the outline of their formation revealed an obvious circle. I knew instantly that it was a ceremonial Medicine Wheel, like the one the dolphins created in the story of the yellow house. I know, I know... it is perfectly reasonable to conclude that this is yet another psychological phenomenon created by the mind, whereby I am turning a random coincidence into a fantasy supporting synchronicity. I certainly concede the validity of that view. However, if you are willing to stipulate that there is a vast, singular divine intelligence moving through all life, then you must concede that the multi species collaboration unfolding in samadhi is likewise perfectly reasonable.

It was a most beautiful ceremony, and that vast intelligence of Spirit provided a comprehensive understanding of its purpose. It was akin to a graduation from a multi-dimensional healing class. Like the dolphin Wheel two years prior, this was a "Completion Ceremony," celebrating the closing of several sacred life hoops. In relation to my personal journey, the ceremony marked the expansion of my lived experience to include unity consciousness. Symbolically, in keeping with our mystical narrative... I went from being between two suns, to then being both suns, to then being the singular Sun that they merged into. Or, we could just as easily say... from the awakening of divinity within, through the dance of the Ishta Deveta, to the divine merging in unity. And just for good measure... from the activation of the transcendent "root" and "branch" systems, to their powerful stabilization and connection, to the merging into full "treeness" and collapse into the infinite spiritual heart.

The ceremony also marked the completion of a specific Earth healing. Spirit presented this component as the fulfillment of a particular mission that I was engaged in for the Earth, despite being only tangentially aware of it. Apparently, I had just unwittingly completed the mission. In so doing, I had employed a multidimensional healing method that we may loosely refer to as "land divinization." I say "loosely," as I am certain that there is no such thing as non-divinized land! Anyway, it's just words to describe a movement. The basic premise is that every high vibration, Shakti-infused step on our sacred Mother Earth is a transcendent point of energy transfer, in one or both directions. For this discussion, the flow moving into the Earth is of primary relevance.

In phase one, I had pounded the beach for two years following my energetic awakening, thereby facilitating the Earth's receipt of new divine frequencies. Hence the phrase "land divinization." As you know, the beach had become holy ground for me personally... it was the setting of the mystical foot stigmata and where I had been graced with a Divine union. In the second phase, I had done the same energetic work on the mountain, sharing my rapidly rising frequencies. It too became personal holy ground, and featured the mystical hand stigmata and a Divine union. Phase three... the mystical tumbling of the Rock of Truth down the mountain, through the canyon, and into the sea... served to multi-dimensionally link the two sacred sites and thus divinize all of the Earth in between. From a more celestial perspective, I connected the physical Earth to a higher dimensional aspect or "grid" by embodying high vibratory states of consciousness at each site. Symbolically, the triumphant return of the Dolphin Christ was a cosmic game of "connect the holy dots" on the divine grid. And lastly was this sublime ceremony, of which I now write, marking the completion of the mission. Of course, the ceremony appropriately took place the first time my feet hit the sand since facilitating the connection. There I sat in ecstatic samadhi on the beach, immersed in the intoxicating divine benediction. The bliss and tears of infinite beauty were there.

We have one more mystical tale in this dynamic cluster of profound samadhi states, as I continue to be transformed and prepared to engage with higher frequencies of source energy. Again, I feel compelled to address an issue of growing relevance before proceeding. It regards the place of religion in my particular awakening story. Despite the obvious religious component of the narrative from the outset, I'd like to further contextualize the use of religious language and symbolism. We've already opened the discussion with an explanation of the Ishta Deveta, but I would like to add a little more to it. For what it's worth, I consider myself deeply religious, but do not associate myself with any particular tradition. I simply consider myself a mystic as previously defined, and there is a mystical element in nearly every religious tradition, some more deeply hidden than others. In that sense, I am a Christian mystic, a Sufi mystic, a Kabbalist, a Yogi, a Tantrika, a Daoist... and so on.

I consider religions to be like the individual facets of a gemstone, a single diamond that represents the supreme essence of the divine. And though each facet is an individual expression with unique qualities, each provides access and opportunity to the same singular core essence, and ultimately the same divine union. They are like archetypal streams of energy that offer different paths home to Source, depending on the aspirant and the innumerable factors and conditions imposed by life. One might be better suited for devotion and another for intellectual study... or service, or meditation, or ritual, or austerity, or renunciation, etc. Yoga as we know it has many such paths and approaches, and in this light I consider the various religions as like forms of yoga. After all, the words "religion" and "yoga" mean essentially the same thing and share the ultimate goal of divine union.

All spiritual awakenings ultimately converge into a single infinite point of union, and any number of metaphors, symbols, and images can provide guidance and revelations on the mystical journey. For example, my next story could be structured around the discovery of Jerusalem within, or the battle of the inner Gijad, or the realization of one's Buddha nature, or the Self, or the Emptiness, or the Fullness, or even a discussion of the quantum unified field. These are all just signifiers of a single, universal, transformational process that is the true subject of any awakening. Finally, if you happen to be allergic to the word "God," for which there are a number of justifiable reasons, please substitute whatever word or phrase resonates with you as indicative of that ultimate divine essence or power. I will spare you a large list of potential alternatives...

That said, as is blatantly evident, it is a Christian template and symbolism through which my personal story would unfold. The Jesus connection, Christ union, and Cross imagery have already been integral to my awakening. As the stabilization and embodiment of divine energy kicks into high gear and things get exponentially more "mystical," I must lean even more heavily on religious metaphor. As consciousness expands, such language becomes increasingly the best way to convey the inner journey, and how it manifests in the phenomenal plane. While the events and symbols of the Crucifixion and the Cross may be replete with gruesome imagery, this is in no way intended to reference or highlight a tale of horrific suffering, but rather a joyful one of utter compassion and Grace. It is nothing other than an epic Love story of redemption and revelation. This chapter is called "The Blood," and now with unapologetic fervor, our next story will tell you why. Time to pour it on, pun intended...

For several days following the dolphin merging, I enjoyed a brief energetic repose and slipped in several good nights sleep in a row... a rare feat. On Friday, I felt a new wave of energy coming on, and it would slowly but unceasingly build for several days through the weekend. By Monday, I was so charged up that I didn't leave the bubble for fear that I was not presentable! When I lay down that evening, one week from the last dramatic episode, I would again be filled with the Holy Spirit and sent into an explosive state of samadhi. Not anticipating sleep, but wanting a little rest, I lit several candles, flopped on the bed, and lay down in the throbbing silence. I was relaxed, though the entirety of my body was purring. I recited my "Mystical Service Trinity Prayer," which had been taking shape over the recent months. I have attached the prayer to the end of the book for those interested. It began with editing known prayers so they would feel more theologically accurate for the mystic, and evolved from there. It is a composite prayer to the Father, Mother, and Brother... with each section containing a line offering my surrendered service. Lastly, after each "Amen", I added my own amen... "Thank you, I love you."

While reciting the prayer, Spirit was rising up in response. My whole being was satiated with the sweet, divine nectar of the Holy Mother's measureless Grace. I would be overflowing in minutes and yet the love-infused current gushed ceaselessly. For someone lying still, it was a profoundly dynamic state and I was visibly vibrating from head to toe. "Stay with me Brother," I pleaded in surrender as Jesus' unique signature emerged within. The swift response was clear and direct. Rather than scolding me for even suggesting that he wouldn't "stay with me," my gracious Brother reaffirmed the solidity and everlasting nature of our union, as only He can. Torrents of blissful tears poured out of my grateful heart and every cell in my body was saturated with bliss. I stretched my arms out wide and I was instantly back on the mystical Cross... divinely linked in the heart, and in a state of total surrender.

For the next ten minutes, I lay in silent awe and wonder, while a vast array of downloads, visions, and teachings presented themselves inwardly... too voluminous and fast to recount. Each "flash" of light contained more information than could be processed linearly. There was no time between blasts of data, but I know it was all received and will be retrieved in divine time. There's a sense that each teaching was purposefully provided, and would be shared with a specific person at a specific moment. I'll certainly be present when it happens, but it will be effortless... Spirit will draw the person to me, and then draw the medicine out of me. This already happens all the time.

The final teaching uniquely came out in real time, and lasted about twenty minutes. "I" or "We" spoke it aloud passionately, and it was called "The Bliss Of The Cross." It was profoundly beautiful yet I recalled very little, as evidenced by the concurrent journal entry. It did address the paradoxical nature of the title... as I was actually blissfully on the mystical cross and therefore in a position to do so. My only other specific memory is likening the hymn lyric "Let Earth receive her King" to the insertion of the Cross into her land. The powerful current of yet another extended samadhi had reached a glorious peak by the end of the spontaneous sermon, and when I closed with "Amen," it went supernova again. There was a flash of inner white light of unspeakable brilliance. My field expanded into a boundless sphere so luminous that it could be seen from space, a view of which I was mystically gifted. And then, as it happens, the entire cosmos was swallowed by its radiance and all creation was encompassed within. I recall saying, "I am that... I am... I... am." One might fairly assume that I am being overly dramatic, but I know absolutely that I'm not being dramatic enough.

The vibratory current was at an all-time high and my body was able to stably conduct the flow. I was securely fastened to the Cross, nailed and tied, and my inner vision became more active than usual. I could look down and see my body and the Earth below... and every few seconds, as if on a loop, I watched a nail get pounded in or the spear pierce my heart. There was no pain, but my physical body actually flinched with each strike. Blood was everywhere... gushing, spraying, and draining onto the Earth. I watched the blood seeping into the dirt and my awareness magically followed its flow beneath the surface. Joy burst forth from my heart in witnessing the rivers of holy, redemptive blood flowing into the sacred Mother. The infinite root system of the Tree of Life was healing the Earth from within, filling its rivers and oceans, destroying all obstacles in its path, and bringing salvation to the planet itself. The unceasing fountain of redemptive blood, with its sacred transformational DNA, was reconciling the Earth with her Divine source, and reclaiming her for the Kingdom of God. A conical energy vortex accompanied the flow, birthed at the source of the blood and widening into the Earth.

That's just the half of it... literally. The mystical vision expanded to include a symmetrical conical vortex, again originating at the infinite blood source, but now pouring upwards into the Heavens. Unlike the deep rich red of the Earth bound blood, the heavenly flow was ethereal starlight blue. As the "root system" below, the upward "branch" system was filling the rivers and oceans of the cosmos and beyond... rippling, expanding, and healing. Beholding this magnificent divine reconciliation is the "Bliss of the Cross." Obviously, in this symbolic expression of healing, it's all about the blood. As perverse as it may sound, for the ecstatic mystic on the Cross, this can only mean one thing... more blood please! I hesitate to expound on how this theme further manifested, but the glare of authenticity demands it. I called out emphatically to be re-nailed with fatter spikes, invited the spear to pierce the heart anew and add one on the other side for good measure... anything to produce more blood. "Pound the crown down on my head," I insisted, knowing that the thorns are thicker near the base and wider holes would pour more redemptive blue blood into the cosmos. I even suggested adding thorns so there was less wasted space between the punctures. I know, I know... but one man's delusion is another's divine intoxicant, and ultimate expression of devotion and surrender to God's holy Will.

I had now been in this transcendent state of samadhi for over an hour and could sense the physical weariness of maintaining such a high vibration, but there was no let down. I launched into a second recitation of the Trinity Prayer, slowly and methodically. My heart was pounding and my chest heaving as I muscled deep heavy breaths in and out of the body, still fully immersed in ecstatic rapture. Exquisite teachings and expositions of every line poured forth after each verse recited, and included visual imagery to capture the totality of meaning. When I was finished, I added an additional closing "Amen," to punctuate both the prayer and the entire mystical session. I began feeling back into my body and patiently rose to my feet. After a few minutes, I closed the evening by dropping back to my knees and bowing in prayer, my cupped hands filling with real tears and mystical blood. I washed the Divine Mother's feet and dried them with my hair. In gratitude She filled the universe with her immeasurable Grace.

The Disciple

AND SO THE stage was set for the next phase of the divinely orchestrated unfolding... and I'd like to emphasize that point again immediately... "Divinely orchestrated." I have not lifted an intentional finger
to drive the action of this awakening journey since day one. It began
and remains a fully spontaneous affair. I had never sat in meditation
or sought transcendence a day in my life. In fact, I was oblivious to the
reality of a full energetic awakening that allowed for consciousness
to expand into its multidimensionality. When the Goddess, Shakti, or
the Holy Spirit emerged in my heart, I instantly surrendered. There
was no impulse for me to grab the reins and control the situation. The
inner guru was clearly and necessarily running the show from within,
with her vast divine power and intelligence. By now the body was accustomed to regularly being in powerful states of samadhi for extended periods of time. It was handling the "juice." And in this dynamic
state of consciousness, multiple lenses of perception were open and
accessible simultaneously. Despite the relentless bliss, I was wakeful,
alert, and clear-minded. My transformed body could handle the vast
divine energy, and now it was time to see if it could be expressed and
lived into the world. Could "I" move around and function in society,
so as to be "instrumentalized" into service by the Goddess, to pour
Her holy Love into the manifest world.

The end of 2020 and the beginning of 2021 would be the time-
frame for this surrendered disciple's next set of lessons and teachings.
Predictably, Spirit would waste no time administering the first test. I
include it both because it happened the day after the bloody Cross

revelation, and because it illustrates how I got off to a rather shaky start on this new phase of the journey. Our narrative now continues with me heading to the beach to ground in the Earth and further process the events of the prior mystical evening. I had my journal in hand to document what I could while the episode was still freshly in the forefront of my awareness. I arrived at the sparsely populated beach and set up my blanket in my usual area, away from where people generally gather. It was a brilliant morning. I sat facing the sparkling water, watching and listening to the rather large waves crashing on the shore. The resulting delightful mist of Mother Ocean was kissing my face, and is one of my favorite sensations in this blessed life. After enough time for my legs to get numb, I closed my eyes and began to bring back the radical Cross unfolding. In minutes I was jettisoned into samadhi anew... and it's always new. Just calling it to mind was enough to trigger the immense surge of current.

In the blissful rapture I began calling out to John the Baptist, whose image quickly appeared to my inner vision. It was both clear and familiar, and I recognized his unique vibratory signature. We have had our own little relationship brewing on the side during this awakening process, usually at the beach and involving ocean baptisms, but not everything makes it onto to the pages of this book! There was a mutual recognition of the magnitude of the Cross revelation, and he opened and extended his arms invitingly. The gesture included the imperative to come greet his presence in the water and be baptized to mark the occasion. I communicated that I didn't think I could physically make it in this extreme vibratory state, not to mention that I had no feeling in my legs. I know I was heard, but it didn't seem to matter. Completely independent of my personal will to remain seated, I beheld my body start to move. It struggled slowly to its feet where it remained momentarily until the wobble minimally stabilized. Then "I" began inching my way towards the water, just slowly enough to avoid toppling over.

I could not stop, for I was not the "doer." There was an invisible tether connecting my heart to John's and I was being reeled in to him.

All I could think was "This is not good... this is a bad idea... I can barely walk... the water is way too rough... I will likely die if "we" don't stop!" My concern was likely shared by a number of beachgoers who were watching the scene play out in front of them. The body kept moving. "Thy Will be done," I said in devotional surrender as my feet touched the water. Suddenly my body stopped and froze in place like a statue, only ankle deep. "Phew," I sighed in relief, as I knew it would have been a dangerous endeavor to keep going. Still vibrant with current, I extended an invitation from my open heart to my mystical brother. "Meet me half way," I communicated with a smile, "I made it to the water's edge!" He did, and I felt his presence emerge within. We turned around, walked back to our spot, and gazed out at the beautiful sea. We sat peacefully together in the benediction of the ecstatic blissfield that enveloped the Earth.

Over November and December I would get my "sea legs" about me and stabilize a higher baseline level of energy. Most of this occurred on the mountain, where I moved about freely, reveling in my love affair with Mother Earth. As I walked around in beauty, I managed the more deeply expanding and contracting breath of consciousness with greater ease. There were a few encounters with other humans that occurred during rather potent samadhi states, but I was able to interact in a relatively "normal" manner... at least I think so! At the start of 2021, the discipleship would begin in earnest. There were little lessons, teachings, and healings along the way, but I believe the following two stories best encapsulate the essence of this phase of the journey. The syllabus for this multidimensional class would involve fieldwork, learning to operate in the world while simultaneously interacting through multiple perceptual lenses. This included handling the powerful surges of Shakti that would necessarily accompany most relevant encounters. I never knew what was coming next during this mysterious unfolding, but I always felt divinely guided, and therefore ready to face whatever life would present. I am deeply grateful for this invaluable blessing and gift of Grace.

The first story took place in mid January. It's actually two stories that occurred on consecutive days, but only about six hours apart. I view it as a short play with a set change... and a mindset change, for that matter. The first part of the lesson plan happened in the dream state, and the second part in the waking state. I haven't discussed the impact of awakening on the dream state, but it's not primary to the utility of this narrative. I will say a few general words about my experience with dreams. I have had scattered "lucid" dreams for decades, in which I become aware that I am dreaming and consciously redirect the action or change the narrative. In such dreams I take full advantage of the different laws of physics, and fly around with intention. The most striking effect of my journey on the dream state was that my dream character was awakening as well! Even in typical non-lucid dreams, I knew that the energetic transformation was unfolding and it was the subject of nearly all dream content.

And now back to our cosmic course work. In this dream, I find myself in an unknown setting, standing outside amid a small crowd of strangers. I am vaguely aware of a woman in my periphery, but my attention is fixed on a man who had just approached and stopped directly in front of me. His description isn't really relevant, but it was quite distinct. He resembled a seventeenth century ship captain or pirate, and though he appeared weather beaten, he retained a hardy presence. His hand was stretched out as if to gift me something, so I extended and opened my hand to receive it. He placed his hand over mine, they touched, and he left it there. I felt an instant jolt throughout my being and the dream went fully lucid. Not only did I awaken within the dream, but I also recognized the interaction as a healing... as genuine as any other. Shakti poured into and filled every cell in the dream body to meet the moment, just like it happens in the waking state... there was sensationally no difference. Yes, the bliss was there! I was no longer a dream character doing a dreamed task, but rather a multidimensional being entering the dream space to facilitate a healing. I was aware of the sleeping body, the dream body, the witness, and the immense consciousness that was moving into and through the dreamscape to transmit the healing energy. From that most expansive awareness, all of the other lenses were but objects of its perception.

I placed my second hand over top of his with healing intention and love, and felt my energy field surge again and expand out from the infinite core of the heart. We just stood there joined together and breathed, brightened, and radiated. I sensed the woman character drawn towards the growing holy light and then oddly perceived her presence hovering behind my right ear. I sensed no particular identity at this time, but her field quickly grew in luminosity to match mine. Once we were in resonance, I understood that she was not a dream character either, but fully conscious and moving through the dreamtime. Upon that realization, our fields merged and I recognized the Divine Mother arise within. She brought blessings of love and gratitude for my role in the beautiful dream healing. I was again flooded with indescribable bliss... loved from the inside out as palpably as if I were in the physical body. When I awoke from sleep that sacred benediction was awaiting me in the waking state, having already filled the space. Dream or no dream, it was a profound state indeed and unique in my experience to date. I was open to and operating through multiple dimensions of consciousness... and, to my delight, I was involved in facilitating a healing. Not bad for the dream state portion of the lesson. Let us now turn to the second act, which would play out in the waking world amongst the other humans!

The next day, only a handful of hours later, I was drawn to the beach for some grounding and a warm soak in the sun. I sat and gazed out at the glory of creation. Within minutes I found myself in samadhi, filled with a refined energetic bliss throughout. I communed lovingly with the sacred Earth. We exchanged and harmonized our frequencies until I was but another cell of her body. I was gifted a cosmic view of the entire beach covered with sparkling minerals, of which my form was just another. I watched its radiance grow in intensity until it mystically encompassed all of creation. In that timeless instant I held the entirety of the manifest world within, and yet was simultaneously in every individual aspect. Yes, I know... I fully understand how far out and paradoxical that last sentence presents... but so it is. Over the recent months of dramatic episodes, I was getting accustomed to calmly abiding through these explosive moments of expansion. I dare say there was a strange element of normalcy arising around dynamic shifts in consciousness. I remained fully rooted in my physicality, though my lower body had gone numb and I couldn't tell where the Earth left off and I began. I also perceived the growing noise around me as more people arrived and settled in. Happy screams of children from the water's edge punctuated a constant stream of shorebird conversations. I was fully present in the moment and aware through multiple lenses of perception. I bathed in the breathtaking beauty, which takes on an indescribable divine glow in such states of consciousness, as if all the Earth were sprinkled with a sacred fairy dust.

Then a woman walked by and sat about ten yards away. She looked to be about ten months pregnant, as if she would give birth any minute. She had that familiar expectant mother glow, which must surely involve some of that aforementioned sacred fairy dust. "I" was immersed in the beauty of which the woman and her baby were now a part. The tears always present when the Holy Spirit is so enlivened, streamed down my face. Spontaneously, I telepathically addressed the unborn child. "It's so incredibly beautiful here," I offered, "You're going to love it! You are blessed to be coming into the world right now, at this amazing time. I can feel how much your mother loves you... you are very lucky." I wondered to myself if it was a boy or a girl, and the unborn child responded immediately... "I am a boy." I acknowledged him and said that he will behold the amazing beauty for himself very soon. Then, still in telepathic communication with the boy, I was engaged from a higher realm. In a flash, Spirit transmitted a "download" clearly expressing why the unborn child and I were brought together, and my role in this unfolding operation of a Medicine Wheel beyond my vision.

I was to connect to this boy just before he was born, which I had already done. Spirit wanted this multidimensional communion to be as freshly in the unborn child's mind as possible, to support his "awakening" at a very early age. I was to tell him this purpose directly and then just sit in beauty with the boy for as long as the connection lasted. During this mystical exchange, perhaps for a little extra credit during my cosmic fieldwork, an acquaintance walking by recognized me and said hello. To my own astonishment, I managed a nod and semi audible return greeting, without dropping the other connections. As directed, I told the boy why we were in communication. I added that the only present difference between us was that I was getting my oxygen from the air, and he was getting his from his cells. And while most people forget about their multidimensionality when they "hit the air," it needn't be the case... I was direct proof, because I was breathing air and with his unborn presence at that very instant. We sat in sublime silence together, taking in the glorious inner and outer beauty. My being was filled with bliss and light, and tears continued to stream down my face. After about five additional minutes our connection ceased, and the lion's share of my awareness slowly and steadily moved back into my physical form.

In keeping with our classroom analogy, I would be administered the final exam for this course in early February. Again the setting would be the beach, where I was spending an increasing amount of time reading, journaling, and grounding. On this day, having established a sweet communion with Mother Earth, I pulled out my journal to document recent events. When I flipped it open, I was drawn to an earlier entry and began reading of the profound lessons, healings, and ecstatic states that have unfolded over the previous months. Predictably, I was flooded with divine current. In short order I was throbbing with vibrant Shakti in every cell, and was unable to operate a pencil. I closed the journal, sat upright, and stared into the infinite beauty. After some time, my attention was jolted out of its ethereal splendor by a growing need to pee! Normally I would have just gone home, but I didn't want to leave yet, and was definitely feeling a little too "cosmic" to operate heavy machinery. I decided to traverse the quarter mile stretch of beach to the bathroom. The sand would be a challenge to my stability as I remained in a potent state of samadhi. I would have to walk with great care and attention.

I decided to pray my way there. Head down, reciting the Trinity Prayer under my breath with deep gratitude and devotion, I slowly and methodically moved one step at a time. I had made it most of the way when I reached the place where some stairs led down from the parking entrance driveway. When I passed by, I was speaking the prayer verse, "May I be an instrument of that holy Will." As the words left my mouth, I peered up the cement staircase and saw a homeless man seated about ten steps up. He was using both hands to adjust the position of his left leg only a few inches... the agony and pain on his face was obvious and jarring, and it swept through me like a haunting wave. I knew without a doubt that Spirit had orchestrated this encounter to do some healing work, and that this synchronicity was a divine call to action. A corresponding energetic surge arose in my being, only now I was a couple of steps beyond the staircase. The bathroom was dead ahead and my bladder was weakening! I resolved to continue to the restroom, and upon my return I would engage the man, though I knew not how.

When I got back to the steps moments later, I stopped, turned, and looked up. The man was on the same step, but had managed to stand upright and was leaning against the steel railing. Our eyes met, my mouth opened, and I spoke. "Hi brother... Are you hurting?" I awaited a response referencing his leg. "Yes," he fired back in a warning tone, "My heart hurts...my heart hurts and I'm very angry!" I spontaneously replied, "Well, it just so happens that I am a heart specialist... May I come up and talk with you for a minute?" After a brief pause, he said hesitantly, "Ok... but I'm very angry!" I ascended the staircase slowly and calmly, so as not to be threatening in any way. In the thirty seconds it took me to get up to him, my brother let loose a frantic, disjointed monologue of fragments to fill the space... "My heart hurts... my dead relatives... the voices... this land here... the voices don't stop... I'm angry!" It was like he was mentally and emotionally hemorrhaging. I recognized it as an acute trauma. There was too much psychological dis-ease to address any particular element, so I went right for the root to try and stop the bleeding.

I stood right in his face and said, "Look into my eyes, brother." I was soft but insistent, and repeated the request multiple times. He struggled to comply, making several attempts, but his eyes kept darting around and his head kept moving. He couldn't connect for more than a split second. "Come on, brother... Right here!" I said more forcefully, gesturing with my fingers. Suddenly, he locked eyes with me... his various erratic motions ceased and we were in stillness together. All the while my frequency was at a fever pitch, my body saturated with healing current as the divine light moved through us. I calmly spoke for several minutes, holding his gaze and empowering this heart space that we were now sharing. "We are now connected at the heart," I said... "Heart to heart... beyond the reach of the mind and beneath all your stories and suffering. Through the eyes we can cut through it all and now my heart is speaking directly to your heart." The peace in this still space was evident, and I could see some relief in his eyes. "Do you feel it?" I asked. "Yes," he said, and then repeated his answer several more times. We were beneath the content of his monologue and his whole being had softened. The powerful beauty of the moment spilled tears down my face and over my smile.

Suddenly his gaze was ripped away, despite his clear effort to hold it. His head jerked violently and his eyes independently shot different directions, before completely rolling back in his head. I was looking at the backs of his eyeballs. He remained right in front of me... grunting, contorting, and trying to look at me anew. "It's ok, brother," I repeated softly, "Come back, brother... look at me brother." After about thirty seconds he stopped shaking and his eyes settled. We locked back in and rediscovered the stillness together for another minute. Maintaining our fixed gaze, I knelt before him and reached my hand out towards his left knee. "Is your leg ok?" I asked... "No," he said... "May I?" I asked... "Yes," he replied. I placed my hand on his knee in hopes that Spirit would do something for my injured brother. His limb was completely taut, inflamed, and looked and felt more like a tree trunk than a leg. The tears of beauty took on an additional flavor of suffering and compassion.

"I'm gonna go now, brother," I said, sensing he was growing antsy. "But I'm gonna take a little bit of your pain with me, and leave a little bit of my heart with you. Your stories will come right back, but now we've seen together that they come and go... the peaceful place we shared in the heart is always there underneath it all and available to you. Just keep your heart open... that's your only job... keep your heart open." I stood up, gave him a smile, and a little nod of gratitude. I turned and descended the staircase in silence. When my foot hit the sand I heard a soft, sweet voice say "Thank you, brother... thank you... thank you." My heart overflowed and tears of love infused joy spilled onto the Earth. I cried my way back to my blanket and collapsed... So profoundly blessed am I. When I lay down that night, Spirit further clarified the smaller lessons and core teaching of the mystical healing encounter. In short, the power of the Christ light entering his heart had made him uninhabitable for an entity filling his head with voices. It fought to remain by unlocking the eye gaze, but was ultimately no match for the divine power present. The entity was forced out when we reestablished our connection and locked eyes a second time. This dramatic multidimensional experience was totally mind-blowing, completely unexpected, and a miraculous divine gift. My heart lay joyously open, as suggested by this contemporary journal entry: Oh, Dear Beloved... The unbridled joy of my only prayer, answered divinely and powerfully... "May I be an instrument of that holy Will"... "Yes, my Son."

In the light of the increasingly dynamic mystical encounters and frequent powerful states of samadhi, it was evident that my awakening journey remained at full throttle as it began. Despite the constant element of mystery and spontaneity, a clear trajectory was revealing itself in the unfolding process. Having stabilized and integrated higher frequencies, I was now facing a series of challenges to learn how to interact in the world anew. Spirit was guiding and teaching me to operate multi-dimensionally, and to facilitate the transmission of healing light and energy to other beings. It was a most magnificent journey, and I was being blissfully lived and loved beyond measure. In navigating through the events of the above stories, it seems that I had shown enough mastery to pass this particular class. I even employed the "eyes" and overcame my reluctance to "use our hands," as Jesus had emphasized. Another inflection point on the sacred journey had been reached, and on the late February full moon, there would be a mystical "graduation" of sorts, marked by an Initiation Ceremony.

To appreciate the full flavor of this event requires the telling of a brief back-story that occurred a few days prior at the beach. I was several hours into a lovely day of reading, walking, and sunbathing. It was a glorious day, and yet there were very few people on the entire beach, and no one within a hundred feet of me in either direction. I looked up from my book to see a man climbing down the rocks nearby from the coastal highway. I was immediately struck by his appearance. He looked shockingly like Yogananda from the cover of his autobiography. The resemblance was so uncanny that I was convinced they must be related in some way. Also surprisingly, with the vast empty beach during a global pandemic, he placed his towel about eight feet away without blinking an eye... directly downwind and alongside of a mask-less stranger. He paid me absolutely no mind, while I was utterly transfixed by his likeness to the great Yogi. He pulled out a book, which appeared to be religious in nature, and was quickly engrossed. I returned to my Hymns of Divine Eros by St. Symeon, and we read together for about half an hour before it was time for me to leave. All the while, he seemed to never consider my presence.

When I got to my car I was startled again. My car was up on the street and there wasn't another car within fifty yards, except the one parked right on my bumper! As I neared, my first thought was that is so like Yogananda's twin to have no spatial awareness! And it was definitely his car... I could smell the incense on approach and the dash was covered with stick holders and various Deity statues. The particularly large Ganesh was adorned with multiple garlands and beads to match the ones that hung from the mirror and doorframes. There was absolutely nothing subtle about his vehicle! I smiled quizzically and drove home. His visage would stick in my head that evening, but then slip into the illusory past. I experience various synchronicities and mysterious events like this on a near daily basis, and normally this wouldn't even merit a journal entry. However, the odd nature of the encounter and the Yogananda connection serve to tie it to the following story. Days later, under a full moon, a mystical initiation would unfold, harkening in the next phase of the awakening journey.

I stepped outside that night, as I often do, to check out the stars and see where my homemade constellations were currently positioned. I always greet my various plant and tree friends first, who resemble and embody various sacred energies. There's Buffalo (tree), St. Mary (plant), St. Francis (tree trunk), and Bear (tree). Sadly, since the time of this journal entry, Buffalo has also become a tree trunk. Bear is the largest tree in the area, and its foliage reveals a magnificent profile of a bear head gazing up at the heavens at the same stars as me. Bear and I have been in "hibernation" together for the last few years while the dramatic transformation has been unfolding. We exemplified bear medicine in withdrawal, introspective and in a larval or cocoon phase. On this night, when I looked up to address my friend, I was immediately startled and blurted out, "Bear is awake!" Having been trimmed last fall, there was ample space between leaves and branches to see some sky. At that moment, the luminous full moon was fully visible and located exactly where Bear's eye would sit in the head. Da Vinci couldn't have placed it any better. "We are awake," I declared knowingly, "Our hibernation is over!" After a few speechless moments of reflection, during which a confirming flow of Shakti coursed through my body, I stepped back inside.

Once inside, I sat on a cushion on my studio floor in my new normal position, in the East of the Medicine Wheel. I typically light several candles at night, but auspiciously, this night was an exception. I flipped off the lights as I sat down and was immediately startled and captivated. Again, it was instigated by the full moon. It shone through my skylight at a perfect angle, illuminating a single object... the kata that my sister has let my steward over the last few years. It is a shimmery, silvery fabric worn over the neck like a scarf or academic honorific. It had been blessed and given to her directly by the Dalai Lama on his most recent visit to Buffalo. In the light of the full moon, it was absolutely luminous and was seemingly the only thing in the room that was reflecting any light. It abnormally stood out... somehow shining more than it "should." Another powerful wave of divine Love surged through every cell of my being, and then filled the entire space with its immeasurable benediction.

I sat for a few minutes in tearful bliss as the holy kata called to me, drawing me into the center of the room where I knelt before it. This happens to leave me facing Yogananda's position in the Medicine Wheel, the great Sage who has been a personal teacher and guide throughout my awakening journey. "Of course, Yogananda's position," I uttered. Instantly, the being we can call Beach Yogananda appeared in my mystical vision... smiling warmly. Remarkably, concurrent with his image, I was timelessly filled with an inner knowing of what this episode marked, and what I was to do. Though the awakening journey is endless, I had reached such a place to where I was being "formally" initiated as a spiritual teacher, guide, and healer. I had sufficiently embodied the transformational frequencies, such that I could simultaneously access multiple lenses of perception while still firmly grounded in the physical plane. This represents the reconciliation of the absolute and the relative... the eternal and the impermanent... the vertical and the horizontal... and the divine and human aspects of our true nature. This is Yoga, and is necessary for a disciple to be initiated into divine service as a teacher and healer. This is my singular purpose moving forward, and a most profound blessing. Of course, one is forever and always a disciple, whether one is aware of it or not. This alone brings a divine richness and sacred quality beyond description to every life.

I was to lift the kata before me, bow my head, and move it through its "gateless gate." In donning the kata I was accepting the immeasurable honor of being a servant of servants... helping to guide the hearts that come before me to the revelation of the "Kingdom of God" within all beings. As the Gnostic Gospel of St. Thomas describes, it is "Spread over all the Earth, but unseen by man." But no need for scripture here... I know this to be true from direct experience, for I live in that Kingdom now and forever. In total love and surrender, I moved my head through the opening and lowered it around my neck. The confirming, all-pervading response from Spirit was indescribable... and of course, blissful and tearful. I returned to my position in the East and delivered a beautiful illuminating talk on Love, scripted spontaneously by divine Grace herself. Upon completion I returned the Kata to its normal spot and went to bed. I have almost no memory of the Love sermon, though I know its essence will emerge at just the right time during my service as a spiritual teacher.

The Mission

SINCE THE "INITIATION," I could perceive a new level of clarity, energy, and stability. For the next several weeks I had visceral consciousness-expanding experiences nearly every day. On a personal note, I could not have felt more loved or blessed to be alive. My Earth connection on the mountain was so intimate and powerful that I walked her every day, still sprinkling in a couple of beach walks per week. The instant I hit the trail with my bare feet and said "Hi Mother," the communication would begin. We had already established our general methodology in working together, using our divine connection to facilitate a healing energy exchange. It flowed into me to help stabilize the embodiment of the transformational energy, and it flowed into the Earth to accomplish the same thing on a planetary level. The former flow can be considered a means of divinizing the flesh, and the latter flow of divinizing the land.

On my first ascent during this span, Earth and I would begin to further develop the paradigm our healing work together. The activity of our sacred hikes had been well established. In profound communion we danced in and out of our separateness and indivisibility... sometimes offering our unique vibrations to each other and sometimes simply resting in unity. Regardless, every step and contact was deliberate, intentional, and loving. The flow of divine energy between us was blissful and continuous. Our interaction was beautifully symbolized in the "Held, Filled, Lived" mantra that I sprinkled in amongst the constant "Thank you, I love you" repetitions. The sacred Earth was that which "Held" me so lovingly in her embrace, while the Divine Mother "Filled" me with the glorious nectar of the Holy Spirit. Thus

I could be "Lived" by Christ Consciousness, bringing that divine energy of healing Love and Light into the manifest world. This is what I considered to be "walking in beauty." The next mystical unfolding would serve to further integrate these sacred walks with the more fully developed symbolism of the Cross and Blood.

On this day, I was physically struggling more than usual while ascending the steepest portion of the trail. Feeling sluggish and out of breath only five minutes in, I called out, "God, just help get me to the top please." He mysteriously and instantly complied, as if a divine upward wind under my wings had reduced my weight by half. I was now ascending in mindless awe. The sense of relief was then accompanied by a holy vision... that glorious act of service of a man lessening Jesus' burden by assuming some of the weight of the Cross. I burst into tears. They were mostly inspired by beauty, but partly by the shameful recognition that I had been seeking relief, rather than to relieve another. Now I wanted the weight back... I headed up to the ridge, where I would determinedly mount the mystical cross, die to myself, and symbolically bleed out into the world. When I got to the top, I stood facing the ocean through the winding canyon and outstretched my arms in surrender. One thing I had surely learned on the path of spiritual awakening, is that it was all about surrender... in every phase, at every level. I had another bliss-filled, teary, mystical episode.

As I stood atop the mountain there was a further symbolic epiphany, complete with inner visions and imagery. In vibrant stillness with the Earth on the mystical Cross, I was rooted down to her very depths as the "Tree of life," and we were now "rotating in beauty." I rotated in the ecstatic vision of bleeding out the infinite red Blood into the Earth, and the cosmic blue Blood into the Heavens. From here forward when walking, I was "Held, Filled, and Lived." When rotating, I was "Held, Filled, and Spilled." Either way, there was always the action of bringing the healing, redemptive blood into the world. I descended the mountain in an intoxicated state of divine rapture, satiated with the bliss of the Cross. From then on, every day was both Good Friday and Easter. I would ascend the mountain in prayer and surrender, bleed out on the mystical cross, and joyously walk the gospel of rebirth back down the hill. Within this movement, the multidimensional healing work in the Medicine Wheel seamlessly continued... generating it's own magical lessons and healings. My relationship with the Earth was richly intimate, and our sacred communion virtually constant. The lengths to which she would go to communicate or "play" with me only increased in magnificence and wonder. Such great love we share.

Let is forge ahead with this particular expression of a spiritual awakening, as the cosmic narrative continues to unfold. May we first consider afresh a most critical point. The details of this journey... the action of the plot and the symbolic imagery woven within it... are necessarily unique to the mystic presenting them. However, it is the universal transformation of a human being that is of paramount importance. Therefore it is of great potential value to be constantly discovering how the individual expression reveals a universal Truth, and actively engaging how that Truth is at play in your own life. This is largely why the book is being written and offered. Truly, this magical narrative is as much about you as it is about me. And while it may be challenging to comprehend, in essence this is your story, as we are ultimately all just reflections of each other. Now, back to the dynamic unfolding of my personal story, which would take another dramatic, divinely orchestrated turn in early March. On a mountain hike, in profound communion with the Earth, I would be given a mission... a concrete, "go do this" mission!

The walk started out normally... I connected with the sacred Mother, engaged our energetic flow, and "bled" my way up to the grassy plateau in surrendered prayer, leaving a trail of "mystic" DNA in my wake... you know, normal! At the clearing I would stop and "rotate" in beauty at whatever spot the Earth guided me to, which was different each day. I was joyously serving our thirsty Mother from the infinitely sourced fountain of redemptive blood, blessed and grateful to play any role in her healing. As I did so, a red-tailed hawk flew directly above me and seemingly stopped. She was effortlessly hovering on the wind in astounding, motionless stillness. I immediately thought of Sedona, the last time I beheld such a sight, when an eagle hovered above me in this manner and helped trigger the rebirth of the Medicine Wheel. I was hit with a jolt of divine current and then flashed an inner vision of myself in Sedona. It wasn't a remembrance, but rather as if I was mysteriously teleported there in the current instant for a fraction of a second. I was given an inner knowing directly from the heart of the Earth, which I still rephrased as a question to make sure I wasn't making it up... "You want me to go to Sedona and "walk in beauty" there, like I do here? You want to heal the land there, like we do here?" The unmistakable, confirming surge of Shakti almost knocked me to the ground. "Ok, dear Mother" I replied, "Of course I will... I will go!"

I quickly turned and headed up Lizard Lane... I had some "dying" to do and some "blood" to spill. Not even the startling revelation of the mission would distract me from my new favorite moment of the hike! I took the position of the Cross at the top of the ridge and "rotated in beauty," tearfully vibrating in bliss. During the joyful descent, through our exquisite communion, Mother Earth would transmit the purpose of the Sedona mission. Wait! What? How? That makes no sense! Explain yourself! These are perfectly reasonable reactions and questions to this abnormal content. Some part of me wants the answers, too, even though I inexplicably already wordlessly know them. Alas, I really can't help with satisfactory explanations. As is often repeated, language is woefully inadequate regarding matters of spiritual awakening. It can do little else beyond circle around a topic, in hopes that by Grace, the Truth will reveal itself. Mother Earth told me our mission had three components: To heal the land, to heal the ancestors, and to further my own healing. That would be all I received at this time regarding the mission. As far as I was concerned, that was enough. I would go and "walk" and "rotate" in beauty... soaking the land in mystical redemptive blood to fertilize the soil and divinize the Earth for her transformation. Simple.

I made my way down and sat upon Medicine Rock, still in the

glorious state of samadhi that had persisted for the last hour. "So... when are we going?" I queried. "Do we leave tomorrow? I'll do it, but I need to know when I'm supposed to leave. I suppose you'll tell me at the right time. I'll sit tight until then, but I'm in!" Again, as frustrating as they may be, I ask you to accept the fact that the Rock then clearly told me that I was to leave on May 17th. That's what happened. Fortunately for me, because Spirit can use her powerful divine energy to confirm her Will, I was placated as to its authenticity in a way that I cannot share. But it was thorough... I received independent energetic surges to confirm the month, the specific day, and the full message. Such confirmations and validations are of increasing importance, especially because the mystical journey gets more and more incredible as it progresses. Furthermore, it certainly wasn't a trip that I would choose to take myself at this time. We were still in a global pandemic, I hadn't worked in a year, and this mission would cost a large portion of my dwindling resources. From the perspective of a practical citizen trying to survive in the world, it was not a wise decision. From the perspective of one who has been "repossessed by the Goddess," it was the only course of action! I would be going...

Before moving on, we need to have one of our little talks to provide some more context for what is coming. Just as we considered the role of religious symbolism before I launched into the last bloody Cross episode, I feel compelled to discuss the use of American Indian symbols and traditions. While it has already been prevalent in our story, particularly regarding the rediscovery and operation of the Medicine Wheel, it is going to become an even more dominant theme. And who am I to discuss such matters? After all, I'm not an Indian by blood, but a white man born in America to an Italian mother and German father, with all the advantages and privilege that such an upbringing implies. Nor do I even possess the minimal authority offered by being a serious scholar of Indian culture, tradition, and history. What I do possess is solely the product of my direct experiences, visions, and mystical connections that are in part revealed in these pages. I'm using the words and terms in the personal way in which they arose during this natural unfolding, not in reference to any accepted definition or strict traditional understanding.

So, those truly knowledgeable on these matters may notice the resulting discrepancies. The lengthy list may include things such as: that's not what a real Medicine Man does, or that's not how you make a Medicine Wheel, or conduct a ceremony, or consider the four directions, or interact with spirit animals, etc.! Correct... Conceded. I don't know any better. By profound Grace, all of my interactions were inspired, guided, and elucidated by Spirit. It is my sense that adherence to tradition may be less critical as Earth and humanity hastens toward a vast transformation in consciousness. Rather than preserving universal truths by observing the rituals that encode them, we are now called to live those truths directly in our daily lives. What I can say with certainty is that when it comes to divine communion, embodiment, and its expression, it is solely a matter of the heart. One can construct a perfect traditional sacred Wheel on the holiest of ground, but if you do not have love in your heart, its power will be superficial. Conversely, if your heart is truly open and thereby a conduit of divine Love, you can turn a rubber band into a sacred Hoop powerful enough to "move mountains," as scripture attests.

Ok... Let's move on. I had ten weeks until the "mission" and I was ready to roll! All I had to do was show up and do what I do here every day! Of course, I knew the divine timing provided was not to be altered, so I quickly resolved to continue doing the work here on the mountain until it was time to leave. I did book my trip and set aside travel funds immediately, for I knew that I would be going... come what may. The power and depth of my Earth connection was stronger than ever, and our walks produced profound communions, energy exchanges, and healing sessions in the Wheel. The symbolism of the Cross and Blood had soaked into every glorious barefoot step, as I blissfully walked and rotated in beauty. It was during this time that the "blood" theme would be further developed with the string of synchronistic references and "downloads" about DNA. I kept seeing the double helix spiral everywhere, including in cloud formations, tree trunks, water, and even dirt. Additionally, due to the season, there were more sharp brambles on the path, and I was regularly getting little cuts and scratches. "Speaking of DNA," I would say to the Earth as I spilled a few drops of real blood, "Here's a fresh infusion!"

As strange as it may sound, we both liked it. Mother happily drank it up and I joyously filled her cup. I was already flooding her with "mystical" blood, and she knew she was welcome to all the real blood as well. It was a beautiful and rather playful addition to our relationship, and she would respond energetically to blissful effect. On a more serious note, I would be provided with the following understanding regarding DNA. I will begin by saying that I have exactly zero scientific evidence to confirm this information. In some manner, my DNA is now different than it was before the comprehensive physical and subtle body transformation. The body must be necessarily prepared to interact with the transcendent energy of our multidimensionality. This is a natural evolution in physicality and activation of our DNA, in order to both house and bring into manifestation the divine frequencies of awakening. The Earth, from whom we are inseparable, is likewise transforming on all levels relative to her awakening. My blood... with its transformed DNA, mystical or otherwise... is serving her awakening as she serves mine, by anchoring and resonating the higher frequencies on the physical plane. In keeping with our operative metaphor, such blood has been made new, and its redemptive qualities are fertilizing the Earth for her glorious transformation and rebirth.

Just a week into the run-up to Sedona, I would get further instruction about the mission. It would involve a ceremony. During my medicine walks on the mountain, I was getting repeated visions of wrapping my hair around a stick. My only reference to this was that I had spontaneously done so on my prior Sedona trip, when I happened upon a Wheel in Boynton Canyon. I finally acknowledged the images, saying, "Shall I make a Wheel and leave some hair on my trip? A little ceremony to mark the mission?" Profound vibratory confirmations followed. No problem, I thought, all I have to do is show up. I'd be honored to leave some hair/DNA. A few days later, I received another mission update from our sacred Mother. In another series of flashing images, I was shown a collection of items that I was to bring to the ceremony. I noted receipt of the transmission, but communicated that I knew this to be superfluous, as nothing external is necessary for the healing activity to take place. She immediately concurred, but memorably added, "It's a ceremony, after all... Let's have fun with it!" I would adopt that mindset instantly. Little did I know, this was just the tip of the iceberg with regard to what the ceremony would ultimately entail.

Over the next two months, my hiking trip to "walk in beauty" would become increasingly more epic in nature and scope. As the trip approached, Spirit worked diligently to prepare me for the ceremony and its various elements. The instruction mostly came in the form of visions and talks through the Buffalo Spirit portal of the Medicine Wheel. This was fitting, as energetic flows to ancestral lines and Sedona itself had already been established. Furthermore, a primary component of the mission was revealed as "ancestral healing," including my own related lineages from prior incarnations. This healing work had already begun in higher dimensions of the Wheel, and could now be fully effectuated by my transformed physical presence, with its powerful vibratory current.

It was a most magical time on the mountain. The Buffalo portal was wide open and a constant flow of energy moved in both directions. I would hit the trail, greet our Earth Mother, and the Native Spirits and Elders would flood my awareness with their vast presence. It was energetically massive, and I was filled with visions of the various elements of the ceremony. There were a few sacred Elders that were regulars, and one distinct Grandmother who was always present and in the forefront... having clearly taken the lead in this operation. She has the full measure of my love and devotion, and I still "see" her and feel her presence. She even once humorously agreed to make me some moccasins for my battered feet! I presume they'll be waiting for me on the Blue Road of Spirit, but I don't discount her power to get them to me while I'm still alive. Last time I asked, Grandmother laughingly told me she had finished one of them!

The preparatory visions were vivid, concise, and accompanied by an inner knowing of their import. This is how I learned the physical actions of the ceremony and their sequence. For the spoken elements, I was provided a breakdown of the different aspects, functions, and order in an extended real-time download. During a mystical, bliss-filled hour on the mountain, I recited the entire transmission aloud as it came through, for additional emphasis and clarification. There were both pulsing energetic confirmations when appropriate, and immediate corrections when I misspoke or misunderstood. On several occasions I asked specific questions which were clearly answered with a flash of insight or an image. Truly remarkable! I won't go into the details here, as that will be revealed in the narrative of the actual ceremony, but I will share the basic structure: 1) Go to Boynton Canyon and allow Mother Earth to lead you to ceremony site. 2) Construct Sacred Hoop in a very particular manner. 3) Invoke Spirits, Medicine Wheel, and Pray. 4) Plant sacred Central Tree. 5) Speak aloud three declarations associated with three healing purposes of the mission... Clearly, we have moved well beyond the original, simple walk in beauty!

It is now the beginning of May, just two weeks before I am to leave on the 17th. I would drive on Monday, fertilize the lands with some mystical "redemptive" blood on Tuesday, and perform the ceremony on Wednesday. The next day I would walk the fruits of the healing around Sedona, and then I would drive home on Friday. Overall, I was feeling fantastic... vital, energized, prepared for the particular movements, and blessed beyond measure to have a role in this beautiful, divine unfolding. I wasn't concerned about the specific declarative language, as I knew that it would flow out in the moment with no ideation on my part. In the final training days, a spontaneous version of each verbal element would issue forth, and Grandmother even had me demonstrate the physical movement to be employed creating the Sacred Hoop... twice. Other than a little sporadic "performance anxiety" to adequately execute the increasingly complex ceremony, I was absolutely primed and ready to go.

There is one more fascinating phenomena from the final two week period to convey, before launching into the narrative that will essentially consume the rest of this written account. I'll admit that this is really "out there," but it was a profound revelation and genuine sensation on the journey. Therefore, I feel compelled to include it. It has to do with time and timelessness. I may be putting the cart before the horse in discussing this, as the ceremony hasn't taken place yet, but that actually serves to highlight the phenomenon. To facilitate an ancestral healing, or any healing that targets the past, consciousness expands to the point of collapsing time. This brings all happenings into the infinite, timeless present where they can be healed or reconciled. When "released" back into time, the past has now been transformed in some manner, just as the future has. So rather than simply a change in trajectory moving forward, the entire timeline has been altered.

I bring this up to contextualize what began happening on my medicine walks. As described, I had been "seeing" the components of the ceremony during preparatory visions. In an astounding revelation, I irrevocably realized that the ceremony in two weeks had already occurred and "released" a timeless healing back into the past... into my present. I was in a powerful state of samadhi and could feel the ceremony's effect on the Earth under my feet and in the depths of my heart. The sensation was subtle, but global. Strangely, I now had mystical cause to celebrate the tangible result of something that I hadn't done yet! I rejoiced with the Earth and started operating accordingly. Albeit in the future, the Central Tree had been planted in the "redeemed" soil, and therefore it was time to sow the multidimensional Love seeds for the rebirth of the Earth. And so I did. I immediately began issuing forth a new infinitely sourced fountain of the aforementioned "seeds," through the transcendent core of the spiritual heart. Grandmother Wind declared that she would scatter the divine spores over the surface of our sacred Mother. I was to manifest the seed and she would do the rest. My beloved Grandmother who was overseeing events looked on... She smiled and nodded approvingly, providing an assuring comfort that she surely knew was about to be dramatically challenged.

From my perspective, the epic odyssey that is the "mission" would begin in earnest right here on the mountain, as a final mystical preparation and initiation before leaving for Sedona. It would span three days, yet its effect would be timeless. Ok, brothers and sisters, its story time. I present the rest of this ongoing journey, as thoroughly as the limits of language will allow. And one final point regarding language... by now you should be used to the frequent interchanging of terms among the variety of symbolic metaphors in play, so I will mix and match freely. They are just words, anyway. It is the divine vibration they arose from that contains their real power and truth. The words serve the mind and their truth serves the heart. Both are of value to the wayfarer. And so, on with the "awakening" dance, divinely orchestrated and richly woven with phenomena, as lived by this particular mystic.

I walked in beauty upon the mountain on Monday afternoon, two weeks before the big adventure. I connected with Mother Earth as usual, engaging the energetic flow through which we feed each other based on her Will. I made my normal stop at the plateau. Having finished reciting the "Mystic Service Trinity Prayer," I thanked Spirit for helping me with the ceremony preparation and invited any additional guidance. It flooded through... a beautiful version of the "declaration" component, weaving the Christ and Cross elements into the Indian theme with great harmony. The Sacred Hoop includes the Kingdom of Heaven and the reborn Earth. The sacred Central Tree is also the Tree of Life, The Arrow of Truth, and the Cross. Shakti filled creation with her presence and my body coursed with vibrant energy, both resolute in purpose and imminently vital. Once again, I walked up Lizard Lane to mystically mount the Cross, bleed out, and radiate the glory of resurrection. "Dying" in this manner is the daily work of "living" for the surrendered mystic.

Ascending the trail in solitude, I nonetheless had the familiar sense that I walked amongst a vast throng. The land around me felt palpably crowded with Spirits and energy. "Let's all go die together!" I suggested, inviting all present to join my daily ritual. As I neared the top, I strongly sensed Mother Mary and Mary Magdalene at my side. When I stood on the peak, fastened to the mystical Cross, I was immediately flooded with emotion. I could feel the deep suffering of the two Marys, as two energetic streams flowing into my heart. There was also an undeniable power in their resolve to go all the way with me during the ordeal. By their exquisite faith, they knew the tremendous glory of the moment amid the horror. It was a most beautiful expression of divinity to behold. I was totally blissed out, and yet also suffering the pain and crying the tears reflected in the powerful streams of emotion. With my arms outstretched, perceiving Mother below to my left and Mary Magdalene below to my right, I sent them each rivers of "redemptive" blood from the Cross. After a few minutes, I bowed in devotion and started my Easter descent, overflowing with vibrant joy. "Let's go spread the Glory," I told the Spirit throng. It was time to walk back down the mountain, dragging the healing cloak of Christ behind us, with its infinite train... bestowing Grace on all it touches and all those who would touch it in true Faith.

This tale would take a most dramatic, mystical turn in less than a hundred feet. Of course there were no real wounds or blood, but I began to suffer the physical effects of "bleeding out rivers" to the Marys. All of the life force was seemingly leaving my body... my breath labored, my pace slowed to a crawl, and I dropped to my knees on the pavement before collapsing all the way to the ground. I sincerely thought that I was going to die. I struggled back to my knees and braced myself on my hands, head down and breath fading. I was failing physically, and yet throbbing with Shakti's vibratory power, with its usual ecstatic bliss. I wept audibly and offered myself to the Goddess, who was clearly in complete control. I was both stunned and perplexed at this unfolding, as it didn't make sense that I would die after all of the mystical events and preparations to serve here on Earth. Was it all to prepare me to work from the "other side?" Waves of disbelief and sadness crashed over the ocean of bliss. My family flashed in my vision and I felt into the great pain this would cause. "Ok," I cried, "Please take care of my family... Thy Will be done." I was in a state of resolved surrender. My blessed life, divinely gifted, I would give back. My last breath felt like it was in my chest. I released it... now I would either breathe into the Lord forever, or He would have to breathe into me.

To my genuine surprise and relief I was able to draw air, though only the most shallow of breaths. I resolved not to die on the ridge, so I struggled to my feet and called out, "Mother, walk me home and stay with me... either home to the Lord or home down the mountain." I stepped wobbly, less than the length of my foot per stride, and the fifteen-minute descent would take well over an hour. I stopped at the plateau for a rest, but only to collapse again, face down in the dirt. I clutched the Earth with my hands, flesh on flesh, and offered myself again... "It's ok, dear Mother, you can have me." I fought back to my knees and paused, filling my cupped hands with my tears.

The profuse crying and vibrant current never lessened, and I had now been in this powerful state for an extended period of time. I was being energetically incinerated in the fire of the Goddess... of this I was certain, and I knew she could "take" me physically at any time. Again, I battled to my feet and began inching my way down to Medicine Rock. I didn't want to stop moving, but I was impelled to at least make contact. I sat upon her for one minute, for which I could barely gather the strength. Still in a posture of full surrender, I continued to work my way down the hill. I must have received some divine "juice" from Medicine Rock, because inexplicably my physical vitality began to return. Beyond reason, by the time the trail leveled out about a hundred yards from my door, I could nearly walk at full stride. I was bodily ok... but the rest of my being was totally out of whack.

I was not the same person who went up that mountain. My mind was completely muddled... I couldn't think coherently and it felt like my consciousness was out of phase. I was neither here nor there, present or not present. I struggled to carry on a simple conversation or perform a mundane task. I set out in my car to run an errand and had to quickly turn back for safety concerns. I wondered if this state was somehow the new level that I would have to stabilize and integrate. That would be challenging indeed. The confounding condition lasted for two and a half days..."tomb" length of course, in retrospect. Finally, in the late afternoon on Wednesday, I decided to return to the mountain, come what may. Still phased and muddled, I got to the path, put my bare feet on the Earth, and started up. "Hi Mother, I'm back... it's a good day to die. Just in case you thought my surrender wasn't complete, I'm coming up to bleed out. Have your way, Holy Spirit!"

I was instantly flooded with love and gratitude by the sacred Mother... it shot up through my feet and fully enveloped me. Bliss filled every cell of my body and every point in space... a single ecstatic field. I was being loved beyond measure as tears of unspeakable beauty poured out. I had been transformed yet again. There was a new clarity... the muddle was gone, and my "phasing" consciousness locked into harmonious congruence with the Earth and Sky. The vertical column of the Goddess was in full flow, and I reveled in its purity until I was no longer in it, but the very flow itself. There was no separation between her infinite divine energy and me. I was loved all the way up and down the mountain in joyous rapture, and the creatures of the Earth greeted me as fellow cells of our Mother's vital body. A new quality of expansion had been gifted and embodied. In keeping with the rest of the journey, I had been relentlessly pushed to the very edge of my physical limits. I believe I could only have passed through this particular "gateless gate," if I truly thought that I was going to die... and I really did. It exemplified the "surrender game" at its highest level. When it comes to divine communion, there is no such thing as a partial surrender. The dramatic events of this story further propelled me along the awakening path, and would prove to be critical preparation for the upcoming mission. I would marinate in this divine glow until it was time to leave.

On Monday, May 17th, the day had finally arrived. With great anticipation, I drove eight hours to Sedona where the ceremony would take place. I was flying high with regard to vibration and frequency, but was not in very good shape physically. The build up to the trip had been very intense on many levels, and I had not been sleeping much. Also, I had been pounding the mountain at least once a day in my bare feet, which were rather beaten up. During my trip planning, I hadn't realized that this date marked another profound event, my father's passing. It was surely no coincidence that Spirit would send me on the mission on this anniversary of great impact. As a hopeless Cross junkie, I quickly surmised that if this is my dad's Good Friday, then his Easter would fall on ceremony day, and we could celebrate together. I found comfort in this synchronicity. I arrived at 2pm and checked into the lodge. To my delight, my room was arrow-themed, another auspicious sign. After all, the pivotal moment of the ceremony was to drive the "Arrow of Truth" into the center of the Sacred Hoop. As we've said... Arrow = Cross = Tree = Me.

I was far too amped and preoccupied with the "mission" to sit still. As the date had approached, I was having more frequent stirrings of performance anxiety... much like what I call "gig stomach," before taking the stage as a singer/songwriter. Though I knew that Spirit was orchestrating events, I felt a growing responsibility to "come through" during the epic, multidimensional happening! I stepped outside for some air and to take in the amazing view of the red rock formations. While standing there in reflection, I watched three vultures drop from high in the sky and fly straight down and over my head, single file and rapid fire. I took it as reassuring comfort from Mother Earth, who communicates with me through her birds regularly. Shakti rose up in response and the energetic juice was flowing. I hadn't planned anything for this day because I knew I needed to rest, but was strongly impelled from within. I felt an undeniable urge to go straight to the Chapel of the Cross, drop to my knees before the giant Crucifix, and begin this journey in prayer. I did just that... off to a great start. I had forgotten from my previous visit that the Cross in the Chapel was an actual tree... the Tree of Life, The Arrow of Truth, embedded in the

Earth. It included the ropes tied around the arms, which I appreciated. In my initial mystical encounter with Jesus, I had very distinctly felt the ropes. I offered my Trinity Prayer.

I exited the Chapel and began to walk down the winding driveway to my car. Right away, while trying to shimmy by a parked car and some oncoming people, I relearned an important desert lesson... even a harmless looking blossom may stab you! A thorn went deep into the fat of my right hand ring finger. It was a bleeder, and surprisingly painful for such a small puncture hole. I instinctively put my finger in my mouth and it was like I tasted the blood with my whole body. It moved through my total being like a wave, and suddenly everything in the world felt slightly different. "Here we go," I thought, "Blood right out of the gate... let the DNA flow." Mother and I had been sharing a lot of DNA in recent months, an emerging theme on the journey. The irritation of the wound was far outweighed by the welcome symbolic validation... a bloody thorn wound on the first stop, less than a minute after kneeling in prayer. Of course, I also loved that it was the ring finger! It beautifully symbolized the divine marriage... the Soul betrothed to the Beloved Christ or the divine union of Shiva and Shakti.

As you might expect, I was feeling quite vibrant and still had a fair amount of nervous energy, so I decided to make another stop. I would pull over at a nearby trail entrance that I had passed on the way. I parked at a sign that read "Mystic Trail," an inviting name indeed, but not as inviting as the beautiful powdery red sand that covered its opening stretch. My feet were salivating! I ditched my shoes in the car and stepped onto the soft Earth. I was instantly soothed and my feet rejoiced. Slowly I began to ground and harmonize my volatile energy field with the Sedona land. It would take three hours and I nearly ran out of daylight, so I had to double time the final stretch on some rather rough terrain. The real import and value of this stop was blatantly evident... I remained abuzz and exhausted, but now I felt in coherence with the Earth and ready for my mission. As one might suspect based on my history, blood was spilled. My right foot caught some jagged shale and cut me enough to leave a little trail of DNA for my thirsty Mother. Two stops, two wounds... right hand and foot. I figured that I would sleep well after my active day, so I returned to my room and collapsed. I did rest, but sleep largely evaded me again. There was a noticeable current that was already rising up to meet the coming healing ceremony. It was unmistakable... waiting in the foreground.

I awoke feeling surprisingly good on ceremony eve. The current was high, but I felt acclimated to the environment and had a stress free day ahead. My plan was to repeat day one from my trip two years ago, when the current iteration or remembrance of the Medicine Wheel was birthed. I had already hit the Chapel the day before, so I would simply circle and summit Bell Rock and then hike the loop around Courthouse Butte. I wore shoes, as there would be climbing involved, and my feet welcomed the rare extra support. It was a beautiful, picturesque Sedona day. I was in a great mood and in no hurry, so I patiently ambled along. I didn't even have to drive anywhere, because my Lodge was a short hike from the trailhead. I brought a mini single-strapped backpack to carry my water bottle, and I took my journal as well. I wanted to document the prior "Mystic Easter" saga on the mountain before the ceremony took place, when it might get more difficult to retrieve.

I climbed just shy of the top, found a nice shady spot, and began to journal... all the while pausing and taking in the breathtaking view. Climbing down proved to be more difficult than climbing up Bell Rock. I had one precarious slip while just jumping down a few feet, but was fortunately able to steady myself with my hand. If you've been paying attention, you can probably guess that this resulted in a fresh bloody cut on my left palm. Three stops... three wounds... Without getting too deeply into the psychology of why I liked it, I did... very much! I felt a strong connection to the Earth and our mission ahead, and most assuring, the involvement of a divine hand and guidance. The Goddess knows just what this wayfarer needs to stay on task, and was graciously validating events as they unfolded in a manner that I would most surely recognize.

After descending Bell Rock, I hiked the Big Park Loop around Courthouse Butte over the next several hours. I took it nice and slow. I could feel that the physical body had a deep fatigue underneath the vibrant energy buzzing throughout the subtle body. I engaged the Medicine Wheel, as I regularly do when facilitating healing on my medicine walks. It was a very powerful, energetic session. I methodically engaged all the Spirit and Animal Guides before working directly with each being present for healing. And as always, I was healed and blessed along with everyone else. The tears and bliss were there. I went back to the lodge to relax before the big day. I finished the journal entry of the story that I had started atop Bell Rock, and then just lay there... content, exhausted, sore, and with great anticipation.

The Ceremony

IT WAS WEDNESDAY, May 19th. My plan for the day was simple. I would get up early and be among the first to arrive at Boynton Canyon. Then I would walk the trail in beauty, delightfully communing with the Earth until she guided me to the perfect ceremony site. Next I would create the Sacred Hoop according to my weeks of divine visions and guidance. Finally, while in an expansive multidimensional state, the inspired prayers and healing declarations would flow through this luminous, blissful container. Looking back, one could fairly argue that this is exactly what happened. However, it was anything but a simple affair... rather, it was quite the ordeal. I woke up an hour later than I wanted, following a poor nights sleep. My body was noticeably sore and fatigued, but the vibratory current was high upon waking. If I skipped my normal coffee routine, I would still get there nice and early. Despite a little "morning fog," I grabbed my prepared backpack and headed out the door.

The tiny backpack contained the items I was to bring to the ceremony. They were all of personal significance and I considered them to be uniquely Spirit-infused. There was my vintage Ethiopian vest, gifted me in my youth from a most loving soul. The exquisite embroidered cross on the back made it ideal ceremony attire. The Dali Lama kata featured in the prior initiation was also to be worn, and was neatly folded in with the vest. There was also the Eagle feather, the beautiful gift that has already figured largely in our story. It was wrapped in a bandana and placed in a cardboard sheath to protect it during the hike. Oh yeah... and my water bottle. In my pocket, I carried my grandfather's gold cross and a Holy Mother amulet blessed by Mother Teresa. They had been with me for decades, and their spiritual power demanded their presence. Lastly, I had a little stone from the mountain and one from the beach. Each had called out to me to make the journey. They would serve to connect the sacred lands, and it was our shared intention that they would remain in Sedona. The contents of the backpack barely fit... it was quite snug and the quill of the dressed feather stuck out the top of the zipper.

I drove out to Boynton Canyon just northwest of Sedona, to find the parking area already full. Cars were lining the neighboring streets and lots of people were milling about. The first solid wave of nerves rushed through me, as I had wanted to be as isolated as possible. I parked my car about a quarter mile away and took a few deep, clearing breaths. As I intended to be barefoot when possible, I realized that I needed room in my backpack for my flip-flops. Cramming them in now might damage the feather, so I decided to lose the water bottle. I took a few swigs and tossed it in the car. I know, I know... but now it wasn't too tight! I headed for the trailhead with my mission on my mind. I was feeling a bit "off," both a little anxious and now a little self-conscious due to the crowd. I breathed rhythmically, and tried to ground the now rapidly heightening energy. Happily, after only a hundred yards, the trail looked amenable to bare feet. Just what I needed! I sat on a little wooden bench and removed my pack to stash my shoes, and ... OH NO! The eagle feather was gone! It must have fallen out! Panic erupted within. In a crazed state of shock, I race-walked back to the start of the trail and then to the car. I was frantically looking every which way and asking every passerby, "Did you see an eagle feather? Did you see an eagle feather? Did you?" I was a sight ... alarmed and barefoot, scurrying along the roadside. It was gone. Of that I was certain, and I was a hot mess!

I knew intellectually that I was completely overreacting on multiple levels, but it didn't matter at all. The disruptive emotional tidal wave had crushed me and I was swept away into a psychological whirlpool. I had blown it before I had even begun! I had intended to pin a strand of eagle hair to the Central Tree during the pivotal ceremony moment. What's more, I had lost a dear possession that had been gifted me during my awakening journey. Here I was... "spiritually-centered" brother g, long graced with the peace that passeth understanding, and I was losing it! On a positive note, I didn't let the turmoil dictate the necessary flow of action. Despite the internal madness, I kept moving down the trail one step at a time. I had a mission to complete, but my confidence in adequately doing so had been summarily crushed. The many weeks of deliberate preparations seemingly went out the window. At this point I was certain of two things: I was doing the ceremony, and I was the least ready that I had ever been.

With my mind racing, I continued down the path. I was closely watching my steps, as the terrain grew less and less appropriate for bare feet. I moved slowly, so I was being passed from behind and from ahead. I tried to pay the people no mind, but mostly I tried to let go of the feather. After all, I knew that my body was the only thing that really needed to make it to the ceremony. Of course, many of us have likely discovered that "trying" to let go of something is the antithesis of actually letting go. Somehow it would have to happen on its own, before I got to wherever I was going. I must stay in the present and flow onward. The Earth soon assisted. She caught the top of my left foot with a jagged edge and ripped it open. It was the bloodiest of my wounds yet, and she drank in the fresh offering. Upon inspecting it, I saw that my right toe wound from Monday had also reopened. I was now bleeding out of both feet and my left palm was throbbing. Of course, as strange as it sounds, for me this was a timely gift. Blood was a dominant theme on my journey, both literally and figuratively, and I took it as a sign that at least something was going right. In loving devotion, I gave myself fully to our beloved Mother. Four stops, four wounds... both hands and feet.

After a brief stretch, my eye was caught by a rock on the ground that looked perfect for the ceremony. It was roughly shaped like a quarter pie, with a nice right angle. I was to gather four such rocks, that the land would provide, to use in the center of the Sacred Hoop. The four pie quarters would be assembled in a circle, slightly separated to leave a space for the planting of the Central Tree. Perhaps this was the first one... I picked it up and clenched it in my fist. Seconds later, I saw rock number two and clenched it in my other hand. This helped my energy field to some degree, as I began grounding my hands and feet to the land at the same time. My thoughts and emotions were still scattered, but my body was slowly stabilizing. A few minutes later I had all four rocks, two in each hand, as I moved steadily ahead.

As I was approaching a portion of the trail that moves along the edge of an open park, I suddenly heard an exquisite sound. Indian flute music, beautifully played, danced through the space. It was deeply soulful and melancholy... like a solemn dirge or a hymn to Death. It was sad yet sublime, and most importantly, heart-opening. It hit the totality of my being like a wave and fresh tears of beauty welled up to the surface. The current in my body surged, and all the frenetic emotional content arose within to be released. When I got to the clearing I saw the elder Native American who was gracing the canyon with his song. There were about fifteen people sitting in the grass before him, listening attentively. At least a dozen hikers listened as well, and had bottlenecked on the trail just ahead. It was captivating music and felt hugely present in the canyon for just a lone flute. The song ended, leaving an enchanting silence. Noticeably, no song would follow, just as no song preceded it... timely and auspicious, indeed.

There was a simple Wheel in the small area between the park and the trail. It was about twelve feet in diameter, consisting only of four cross-shaped log posts. Their paint was mostly faded... the colors signifying the four directions. There were no other markings or even a circle inscribed on the ground. I, with my exposed open heart, was drawn to it like a magnet. Shakti was now clearly in control. I marched right through the people gathered to the center of the Wheel. All eyes were focused there, yet the self-conscious instincts arising were no match for the Goddess. I fell to my knees near the center, wet with tears and in a trance-like state. It was a combination surrender, plea, and communion with the Earth. I dropped the rocks, bowed down, grabbed two handfuls of dirt, and rubbed my hands together deliberately. I was next to a little thorny bush that was about a foot off center, but a single branch grew out on its own and seemed to touch the core of the Wheel. I immediately started raking my fingers through my hair to collect an ample offering. I got quite a handful, twisted the strands together, and attentively wrapped my hair around the end of branch. I picked up the four rocks, stood up under the watchful gaze of dozens of people, and walked back to the path to continue the mission. Like it or not, I surely provided some tourists with an interesting little story to tell.

I continued along the trail... barefoot, wounded, purging, and exhausted... yet with the growing vitality of Shakti's presence. Holding the rocks in wordless prayer, I awaited the intuition to turn off of the main trail toward the ceremony site. According to my visions, this was the next move. After some time, and having passed several uninviting side paths, the giant red rock cliff face caught my eye... with its "eye." Looking to the right as one moves along the trail, there is a massive U-shaped formation of striated red rocks, hundreds of feet high on all three sides. The large expanse in the middle is a thickly forested area that comes all the way to the main trail, which turns the U-shape into a rectangle. Part of the way up on the middle rock face was a pronounced black oval cave hole, and it literally felt like the stone was looking at me, drawing my attention with its eye. It became my direction marker. I would turn off at the next opportunity and head for the eye. I was looking forward to getting off the main trail and away from the other humans.

I saw a thin path and turned towards the glaring stare of the rock face. I was on the lookout for an appropriate clearing, which I assumed would present itself on this trajectory. The brush was thick, the ground not very level, and the path ended abruptly. But there was no turning back... I put my flip-flops back on and plowed right into the thicket. I was laboring with every step and no clearings were apparent, but I held my line with an unmovable determination. About midway to the rock face another generous DNA offering was made, or shall I say extracted. I was already bleeding from both feet and now had numerous scrapes and scratches on my upper body from the unforgiving foliage. One consistent physical symptom of my personal transformation has been an increase in fluid with the increase in energetic current. Though weak and likely dehydrated, I was generating a lot of saliva and began spitting constantly. I then had a bizarre three minute "cold"... during which my eyes watered, my nasal passages drained, I was sweating profusely, and had a nasty phlegm filled coughing fit. My body emptied in every possible way... yes, that way too. On multiple occasions during the radical purge, I exclaimed, "Have some more damn DNA!"

There was still nothing close to an adequate clearing, and the terrain began steadily rising as I approached the "eye" of the rock face. What had looked so high from back at the trail, now only appeared to be about thirty feet up, and I could see a way to get to it. Also, there was a decent sized ledge by the cave entrance. I thought at the very least, I could rest for a few minutes and scan the surroundings from an elevated perch. I went barefoot for the climb and made my way to the ledge. I removed my pack and sat for a few minutes, having still not discovered the location of the healing ceremony. I surveyed the terrain, looking for a clearing to accommodate my roughly six-foot diameter Hoop, and saw none. The land basically sloped down into little valleys in each direction, and I couldn't see well enough below the dense tree line. I peered at the "eye" behind me. The cave hole was about three feet high, four feet wide, and an unknown depth. It was large enough to enter and it occurred to me that it might not be vacant. I thanked it for being my directional guide, but decided to otherwise avoid the cave.

I noticed that between my position and the entrance was a square foot of beautiful, smooth, red sand... almost a dust. I thought if only the ledge was covered with it, it would be ideal for tracing a Wheel.

Then I saw that the shade of red perfectly matched the shade of my four rocks, and before I knew it, I was spontaneously making a little Wheel. I was physically exhausted, swirling with high frequency energy, and in some "altered" state of consciousness. It was fiercely powerful and there was a perceivable sensation of being slightly out of phase. I issued forth a chant and heartfelt prayer, as I traced a small circle in the dust with my finger. I set the four rocks in place with enough room in the middle to plant the Central Tree. I looked up and there was a perfect little stick for my purposes, the only one visible on the ledge. It was about three inches high and had a hole on the top like a sewing needle. There was a split in the opening, so it could even be pulled apart and snap closed on the hair offering. It couldn't have been intentionally designed any better. I raked out some hair for a good twisted strand, threaded the needle, and wrapped the stem. I held the "Tree" above my head and drove it into the sacred Central Mountain, eagerly waiting to receive it.

What happened when the stick hit the Earth was profoundly mystical, and these words will fail to adequately convey what took place. It was as if the Earth drained vast disharmonious frequencies from all aspects of my being at once, including emotional and mental content. Simultaneously, a massive infusion of harmonious divine current jolted me from within and I was globally transformed in an instant. I was suddenly lit up, empowered, and totally stable energetically. The wobble was gone and a familiar wave of immeasurable bliss flooded every cell of my body. Joyful tears poured out amid a renewed fire and earnestness for the imminent healing ahead. Great Spirit was at the helm, leaving no doubt that I had been "instrumentalized." From the park Wheel to the dust Wheel, the ego identity had fully surrendered. The "doer" of the ceremony, the "Medicine Man" who was there to heal, was no more. It is impossible to explain the lived experience of the death of the "doer." Only one's own inevitable ego death will suffice. But so it was... and so it needed to be, for the purity of the energy to match the magnitude of the intended healing.

I dragged the first two fingers of both hands through the red dust outside of the mini Wheel, and applied two horizontal stripes of "war paint" beneath my eyes. I added a smear from the third eye over the top to the center of my head. I stood up boldly and let out a few mighty calls of "Aho!" I was in an extremely expansive state of consciousness. It was quite "dreamlike" as experienced through the physical body, but there was clear perception through multiple dimensional levels. And most notably, I was being "lived" by Spirit. As such, finally "I" was now more ready than ever for this pivotal moment and sacred healing. Seeing no clearing, I headed down the opposite way that I had come up in order to cover some fresh ground. I zigzagged downward and entered the thicket, seeking both an adequate clearing, and a necessary confirmation from Mother Earth. After only a few minutes, I came across a space just big enough and was drawn to stop. I remained uncertain, as the leaf and brush covered area wasn't totally level. Upon inquiry, the Earth sent a confirming pulse of energy that instantly settled the matter.

I set my pack off to the side, and put on the Ethiopian vest with the Tibetan kata over top. I would have tied the eagle feather in my hair at this point, but it was gone... and it mattered not. I knelt in the space in greeting, and there was one of the four rocks that the land was to provide. I swept the top layer of leaves with my hands and had the other three stones in short order. I was on "non-doer" autopilot, but fully conscious in the activity and vibrant with divine current. I set the four rocks outside the perimeter of the future Hoop. I noticed that a particular tree was just preventing me from making the circle the size I felt compelled to make it. I was a bit confounded. I didn't want to make it any smaller, yet I was absolutely certain that this was the spot. With that in mind, I placed my hand on the tree and asked her what she thought. She responded immediately directly to my heart, essentially communicating the following: Make the Sacred Hoop go right through me... just trace around me with your foot and I will keep the Hoop unbroken. I am part of this ceremony and this Wheel... you stand under my canopy, over my root system, and the ground under your feet is covered with my leaves. That settled that.

A glorious welling up of bliss and tears came with the recognition of this intimate collusion of Nature in her own healing. The tree and I were both ecstatic about her role.

I stepped to the edge of the clearing to begin tracing the Hoop and suddenly heard voices... I had wound up in a spot where loud hikers on a section of the trail facing my direction could be heard. I knew that the reverse must also be true, and this possibility had been a source of anxiety in prior weeks. I was specifically directed that the ceremony must be conducted aloud. Spirit wanted it fully expressed, such that the vocal vibrations would ride the winds of the phenomenal plane. So it was... and it mattered not, for the one who was self-conscious about being heard was also not. I would now make the Sacred Hoop, a full-sized version of the one I had just formed in the red dust.

I won't describe the process in detail, but I created the Hoop as guided by the visions received on my preparatory walks. I traced the circle with my heels, one at a time, moving backwards. Ultimately, both feet would trace the circle in each direction. First I moved around with my body outside of the space, and then I completed the etching from the inside. I was vocalizing a particular chant, which provided the beat that synchronized the fist pounding of my chest with the rhythmic carving of the Earth. My heels dug forcibly through leaves, sticks, and stones... into a rich, dark brown soil that felt sublime on my flesh and smelled of fertility. Upon completion, I noticed that although the land was not totally flat, it appeared that the traced Sacred Hoop at depth was level. The tree and I were pleased, and the embodied energy was blissful, powerful, and operating. The tears were there.

When I stepped fully into the center of the Wheel, I brought the four rocks in with me that would delineate the Central Mountain and receive the Tree of Life. The ceremony itself consisted of three main elements: 1) Prayer and invocation for the gathering of Spirits. 2) Construction of central Wheel and planting of Tree. 3) Recitation of the three "declarations." Much of the ceremony is nearly impossible to recount, particularly the specific language of the declarations. I will do my best, however, to describe the structure, process, and themes of the healings. Of course, it is the lived experience of the mystic that is the primary focus of our narrative and purpose for sharing.

I fell to my knees mid-Hoop and began with an offering of the Mystic Service Trinity Prayer. I proceeded to call forth and invite a vast array of Spirits and Essences, woven with prayer and sacred intent. The list was long and comprehensive. It included the Earth, her Elements, the Directions, the Sun, Land, Rocks, Sky, Ancestors, Grandfathers, and Grandmothers... You get the idea. I next engaged the Medicine Wheel that I use for much of my healing work, remote or otherwise. Resonance was established with my various Spirit Guides, and I would have powerful individual interactions with each one. These communions were joyful, tearful, and heart opening, yet reflected the depth and seriousness of this particular moment in time... with its divine healing opportunity and resulting "timeless" ripple effect. I presented my Grandfather his gold cross from my pocket, and likewise the Holy Mother amulet to the Spirit of Mary Magdalene. I would also have a most profound interaction with my father that I will cherish forever.

The connection to the Buffalo portal of the Medicine Wheel was predictably potent, as this energetic "thread" was a primary focus of the Earth's healing. A massive current of energy and Spirit was pouring through unimpeded in both directions. The previously quiet forest became noticeably louder. Everything seemed enlivened... crackling, popping, crunching, splitting, and falling... as if the vast throng of "invisible" invitees was announcing its presence on the physical plane. I soon realized this and stopped looking around for the sources of all the noises. I was alone in a small clearing in a forest, and yet it was very crowded indeed. In the current state of expanded consciousness, all of the energies present were experienced both within and without. By divine Grace... I was my physical self, each individual element, the totality of elements, and the very source of all the energy at play. There was a magnificent array of dynamic flows amid a singular vibratory coherence. All dimensional barriers were dissolved, uniting the full spectrum of life... from the physical density of the Earth through the borderless realms of the transcendent.

There is one more facet of the prayer and gathering phase that merits a mention, as it involves the infamous vanishing eagle feather. Though it was quickly out of my possession, it did indeed manage to play a starring role in our story... by its mere absence. When I had engaged the Spirits of the Medicine Wheel, I looked to the heavens where Eagle hovers, and thought of the lost feather. "I'm sorry you're not here," I communicated with great affection. I was immediately hit with a joyous wave of energy and heard Eagle's repeated refrain, "I'm free! I'm free!" I could sense the energy taking off, leaving the Wheel vortex, and seemingly the entire multi-dimensional Earth altogether. In a simultaneous mystical flash, I received a "download" that contained the relevant part of Eagle's story. In short, the feather had just to return home to the Canyon before its soul could be free, and so had found its way to me. Interestingly, it was returning home to where this Soul had lived a human incarnation before it's life as an Eagle. So it turns out that we each played a liberating role in the unfolding of the other's story.

The next part of the ceremony was making the small interior Wheel within the larger Hoop. I would use the four collected rocks as I had done in the red dust on the ledge. I knelt before the center of the Sacred Hoop, facing true East, where the bright sun was just above the massive red rock face. My body was humming with energy and I wept in bliss from the sheer depth and power of the vast flow of divine current. I perceived a notable phenomenon at play in the energy swirling about the Hoop, as a direct function of my position. In my Medicine Wheel that has a fixed orientation to my physical body, I am always seated in the East, bringing through Spirit and facing the West. At this moment, that Wheel is superimposed upon the Sacred Hoop that I just carved into the Earth. The land Hoop is oriented to the sun, and is thus rotated a hundred and eighty degrees relative to the Wheel. The East and West poles are reversed, and both sacred spheres are highly charged and activated.

The resulting phenomenon is an infinite energy "feedback" loop, in which I sit in the East facing the East, and the source energy of each Wheel is flowing into the source of the other. The resulting powerer is indescribable. These two source points would then merge and dissolve into each other, in the limitless core of the spiritual heart. For the purposes of the healing, the transcendent and imminent had collapsed into an infinite zero point, through which all energy was manifest. With the eternal so yoked to the physical plane, the timeless healing could take place through the physical vehicle in time. The convergence of the past, present, and future in the eternal now allows for the full thread of a lineage or timeline to be effected instantly.

Back to the story... I marked the sacred center point by inserting my finger into the Earth and grabbed the first rock for placement. As I did, I abruptly felt my physical body begin to crash. It was eerily familiar, for it mirrored my recent collapse on the mountain. The sudden weakness made it challenging to remain up on my knees, and I knew I was in rapid decline. My head bobbed and I felt faint like before, as if all the blood was draining out of my body. My breathing became slow and labored as if I would soon be drawing my final breath. It was clearly the same phenomenon as before, yet I now understood the episode in a different light and there was one key difference. On the mountain, I was convinced that I would actually die, and this time I knew that I would not. I had learned from the prior episode that I could handle the enormous energy that the healing necessitated, though it would push my body to its absolute physical limit. I had been trained for this moment, so I could provide the multidimensional container and portal to facilitate the healing. I wasn't the least bit concerned and continued on at a slow, methodical pace... barely, yet adequately breathing.

I placed the four rocks and looked around for a stick to serve as the Central Tree. Remarkably, but not surprisingly at this point, there was a perfect stick within arms reach. It was just like the ledge stick, with an open loop at the top and about twice its size. Once again I raked my fingers through my hair until I had a nice handful, twisted it into a single strand, and married it to the stick. I pulled my two little stone friends from my pocket, one from the beach and one from the mountain, each about the size of a chocolate chip. I had thought to place them atop the set rocks of the inner wheel. In doing so, I dropped the beach stone and it bounced right into the center hole like a planted seed! I added the mountain stone directly to it. With seemingly all the might remaining in the body, I held up the hair-wrapped "Arrow" in tearful silent prayer, and thrust it into the receptive Earth... into the infinite center of the sacred Central Mountain that was represented here... and is actually here... and is actually everywhere.

Not to sound like a broken record, but what happened at impact is beyond the limits of language. This was the merging or collapse point of the vast, multidimensional flows of energy described above. As for the physical body, it remained utterly maxed out. There was a further refinement that would take place, in which the high frequency flow reached a peak harmonious stability. The status of the dense bodily vehicle was unparalleled in my experience, in flawless rotation and securely rooted to the Earth. Yet it was the profound, mystical impact of the Central Tree on the "light" body that dominated perception. There was a magnificent explosion of glorious light. The infinite zero point, that is the seat of consciousness and the healing portal in the spiritual heart, went supernova with divine white light... like the Sun and the Son. I rose to my feet with much effort, to deliver the ceremonial declarations. I knew now why this was a declaration and not a prayer or petition. Simply stated, I was not seeking a result from source, but rather I was that source in operation. Instead of the posture being "I hope this works," it was "This is so."

The deep sacredness of this healing cannot be overstated. The inspired language of the declarative component could never be replicated, but it was beautiful, poetic, inclusive, redemptive, and irrevocable. I will touch upon the main themes as I continue to describe the course of events. Declaration one was for the healing of the Earth. It is she who dispatched me on this mission, to continue our ongoing healing partnership to midwife her rebirth. Most generally, the purpose is to bring the energy of a higher consciousness field or "grid" into manifestation on the physical Earth plane. Symbolically, "bleeding" into Mother Earth was a holy infusion that did just that. As I walked in beauty, the divinely sourced redemptive blood seeped its restorative essence into the physical realm. The soil, the flesh of the Earth, is thus mystically "fertilized," and her body made ready for the profound transformation of planetary awakening. Purely in terms of energy, the heightened vibratory frequencies of my transforming body were directly infusing the energy field of Earth through resonance.

At some critical point of ripeness and divine Grace, our sacred Mother Earth will be ready to receive the "ascension seeds" of Light, Love, Beauty, and Truth. The growth of these luminous, multidimensional seeds will both anchor and welcome the higher frequencies of "awakening" into her physicality. The ceremony marks this sacred point of ripeness in which it is time to "sow." I was most intimately connected to the Earth, both in divine conjunction for the healing process, and as a singular being. The energy was vast, harmonious, and blissful. Voluminous tears of beauty wet the Earth. When I made the declaration, a new simultaneous fountain issued forth from the depth of our being. In addition to the redemptive blood, now a flow of the transcendent "seeds" shot skyward from our heart... unbroken and likewise infinitely sourced by Spirit. That was it. Grandmother Wind would do the rest, carrying and scattering the divine seed all over the surface of the Earth. I was then, now, and always shall be that singularly sourced dual fountain. There had been a beautiful healing, locally and globally, and I perceived a subtle, but glorious celebration.

The next declaration was for the healing of the peoples and lineages associated with this land, including my own ancestral line. This component goes far beyond the healing of any specific event that took place in time, to include broader cultural and spiritual "dis-eases" in the Native peoples collective. This is an indispensible part of the above land healing work. Though more narrowly focused, these disharmonious energies in consciousness are part of the Earth's subtle body, and must also be reconciled and brought into divine coherence.

I was standing still... a humming conduit of source energy rooted like a tree in the sacred Mother. While beautiful, holy language of love and healing came forth, I brought the ancestral "flows" into sharper focus. These connections had already been established as a part of ongoing healing activity. While the harmonious inclusion of these energies was the prior work, now the ceremony would act to transmute them altogether. Most prominently, the healing was to address the profound collective sufferings that continue to restrict the consciousness of both the people and the planet. The metaphysics of the healing was experienced as follows: The inner sun in the core of the heart, that had ignited with the planting of the Central Tree, coalesced into an immeasurably brilliant, smokeless flame. It acted as a "White Hole," drawing in the vast streams of energy to be transmuted. It was effortless... there was no resistance in the "field," but rather a glorious eagerness to dissolve into the sacred Fire. Floods of purging, blissful tears of release and renewal rained down upon the Tree of Life.

Then the tsunami hit... or more accurately, began. Wave after wave of peak intensity, communal suffering crashed into the infinite flame. I was instantly knocked to my knees by the very first wave, and audible wails accompanied a sorrow so vast that only the infinite heart could contain it. This lasted for about ten minutes, and was undoubtedly the most taxing part of the ceremony on my entire being. It was what I had been "instrumentalized" for... the literal moment of Truth. Other than the visions that served as preparation for the mission, there has not been an emphasis on visual phenomena on my journey. In this case, however, a "slideshow of suffering" would accompany the energy being reconciled. Mercifully it was only about twenty seconds long, but it was horrific... imagery that one might expect to correspond with a genocide. Bobbing my head up and down over the center of the Hoop, I wailed with the Earth and Sky and Spirits in communal cathartic expression. The rock face in the East wept rivers with us. Its three prominent aged-blackened vertical lines, in this most profound mystical moment, came to compassionate life and cried with us all.

Standing in and as this divine vortex was awesome. Such profound darkness and brilliant light were there together at the dissolution point, and yet it was all contained within the expansive blissfied that has no edges. The power and effectiveness of the portal was obvious, and vast streams of energy poured in to be transmuted. During this ten-minute span, the vortex expanded exponentially, until it was drawing the energy of Indigenous cultures to include Canada and South America. The "juice" was high, and Spirit was going for it! When the sacred Fire had done its work, I let out a great sigh as my head dropped over the center of the Wheel. As I did, the kata reached forward with both "arms" and covered the four rocks right under my face. "Ahh," I cried, "The Dalai Lama is here... thank you, brother... that was some healing, wasn't it?" And ... Boom! Before the sound vibration of my question could dissipate, another tsunami crashed into the transmuting fire. It was a shorter version of "Indian" wave, only it was the "Tibetan" wave. It would last only about three minutes, but was complete with genocide grade suffering and some gruesome associated imagery. When that stream ran its course I knew with certainty why the kata was worn and present at the ceremony. The depth and magnificence of these healings, as experienced in the multidimensional Sacred Hoop, is simply immeasurable.

Feeling physically like I had just run a marathon or two, I struggled to my feet to offer the third declaration. Before doing so, while standing in and as this powerful healing field, another spontaneous act occurred. Recognizing the unique heightened vibratory and luminous nature of the vortex, I sent several directed pulses of light through the Medicine Wheel to all who may be served by them. One particular being appeared clearly in the mind's eye... I swiped my hand over the affected area and said, "Let's just be done with this problem once and for all." Like all the healing in the ceremony, it was not a request if in accord with the divine Will. At this quantum instant, there was no separation of "Wills," nor a petitioner and the petitioned. The action of "Oneness" flowed from itself, through itself, and to itself.

The final component of the declaration was related to my personal journey and healing... marking another circle of life, and spiral of life-times. Without a doubt, the most important aspect of the ceremony on my personal healing was simply my participation. This wordless truth required no declaration. There were a few spoken elements that related to my journey. After all, spiritual awakening and energetic transformation are just synonyms for healing, from an expansive point of view. One noteworthy circle of life is that I had managed to arrive at this place on Earth, as in prior incarnations, having awoken to and operating the Medicine Wheel. In this particular life story, it was my Sedona trip two years prior, when and where the Wheel remembrance began in earnest. That metaphysical rebirth was being celebrated.

That auspicious trip also featured the gathering of other "mysti-cal" ingredients and revelations for the awakening process. Having assembled and integrated those ingredients, I was now returning to serve the prepared dish to my "relations" in gratitude. That's basi-cally what I said during the short, spoken offering, but I used corn-bread as the metaphor in the actual declaration. Of course, I am the cornbread and offered myself as nourishment and sustenance. It was another beautiful surrender and manner in which to express our es-sential unity. The bliss was there. The tears were there. The ceremony proper was over, though it is timelessly occurring now and always. I issued a brief chant and prayer of love and gratitude, and stepped out of the Sacred Hoop. Of course, that isn't really possible... for I am the Central Tree, Mountain, and Hoop. I beheld the scene for a few minutes, packed up, and entered the thicket in the direction that I had previously heard voices.

It was a smooth exit. I followed a dry creek bed nearby that led to a small path, which in turn led back to the main trail. The second I stepped out into the clear, open sky I was greeted by the most appro-priate synchronicity. I heard some boisterous "WhooHoo's!" I looked up and saw a man standing at the base of a large rock column about a hundred yards away. He was vociferously cheering on his buddy who had just completed the difficult fifty-foot climb. I noticed him just as he reached the summit and stood up. He let out a huge scream of victory, reached into what looked like a quiver, and pulled out an Indian flute. He began emphatically jamming a celebratory, dance-able hymn. It was like a party, and others in the area joined in the hol-lering. He looked shockingly like that common image of Kokopelli we are all familiar with... he may have even been going for that look as his buddy below shot video. It was a fitting image for the occa-sion, given that Kokopelli plays the "Song Of Fertility," a key theme of the day's events. So my journey into the Canyon was bookended by Indian flute music... the opening dirge and the closing anthem, synchronicity at its finest!

I returned to bare feet, floated back to the car, and drove to the lodge. I was in an ecstatic state of samadhi... the world seemed a luminous dream, and yet there was a vivid clarity and vitality. Tears of beauty were welling up and spilling out all the way back. I'm not quite sure how I made it, but I was back in my room before noon. I made it pitch black and flopped on the bed, in anticipation on an epic crash. Sleep would not come... rather I'd be acutely aware of the vast energy flowing through my being. For the next ninety minutes, I lay aglow, receiving and transmitting. Voluminous light and informa-tion about the ceremony was flowing in both directions. Beautiful lessons and teachings came forth as well as expository downloads about the various components of the mission. Some of it has surely made its way onto these pages. At the end of the cosmic exchange I was rejuvenated, and felt called to go walk some "seeds" around for Grandmother Wind to scatter. Now I know that a clear beautiful day in Sedona is spectacular to all eyes, but when I emerged outside it was like when The Wizard Of Oz went color! It felt like the world had indeed been made new. The physical exhaustion remained, but I was otherwise bursting with peace, love, and joy.

I decided to return to the Big Park Loop and walk around Bell Rock and Courthouse Butte as I did on day one. This time I would walk in the reverse direction and there would be no ascent. It was a glorious outing. Barefoot and at a snails pace, I made the loop in about three hours. To my delight, it was quite windy, with some impressively strong gusts... perfect for "seeding." I walked in beauty, both infinitely sourced fountains flowing, and Grandmother Wind did the rest. Of course, the bliss and tears were there constantly. I returned to my room and crashed until the next morning, awestruck by all that had transpired. I slept for a few hours. When I awoke the next morning, though I had another full day and night on this trip planned, all I could think about was going home. My work here was done and I had no impulse or energy to do anything, not even to simply relax. I packed the car, got a large coffee, and hit the road. As a result of my ill-advised timing, the final two hours of the lengthy drive was a slow crawl through rush hour traffic, in the heart of Los Angeles. I managed to make it back to Topanga, but the end was definitely sketchy, and I was relieved. Divine intervention is a primary theme in all of these stories, and was no less present for the drive that got me safely back to the g-bubble.

Little did I know, there was one more scene in the final act of the epic mission saga, which would occur the next day on the mountain. I got some desperately needed sleep that night, as I had pushed my body to its absolute limit. Upon waking Friday morning, the entirety of my body, being, and world felt transformed again. I was rested, peaceful, energized, and profoundly lucid. It was the same sense of renewal from my post ceremony walk, only magnitudes greater. I wouldn't have thought it possible... let alone what was to follow. I felt an urgent draw from the mountain and danced out the door. I will characterize this Medicine Walk in brief, as its depth is far beyond the reach of language. Given all the bliss, tears, and mystical states described in these writings, this walk would result in the most incomprehensible expanded state of unity consciousness that I would ever be graced with. I'm sure there is some exquisite Sanskrit term for this "flavor" of samadhi, but it too must fall woefully short. The lived experience of that which cannot be signified, simply cannot be signified.

When I got to the trailhead, I removed my flip-flops to greet Mother Earth with my bare feet as always. Right away, I noticed that my feet were still stained with the sacred red earth of Sedona. I had not showered since the ceremony, nor did I have any desire or impulse to "wash it off." (I will not disclose how long I went without showering!) "Hi Mother," I rejoiced, "We did it! And I brought you something!" I rubbed the soles of my feet on our receptive Mother to merge the land and minerals of the two sacred locations. The response was immediate, powerful, and divine. The bliss meter was turned up to ten instantly, and I burst into tears. I was returning to that place on Earth where she herself had enlisted and prepared me for our joint mission. I had gone "all in" for her... accepted, trained, and executed the ceremony. Now, in an overwhelming expression of gratitude, she was going "all in" for me... she and a spectrum of multidimensional life. Spirit always graces me with great bliss in association with some lesson or healing, but here she made it abundantly clear that this was a "thank you," as well as a validation of the divine result. This heavenly benediction enveloped me for the entire ascent, amazingly getting progressively stronger as I walked.

By the time I reached the top of the ridge I was wailing with bliss and beauty, and vibrating at a glorious frequency. It was a total love fest. I was crying, "Thank you, I love you" with every step, and in response Spirit embodied me with the very vibrations that those words signify. What started at level ten had completely shattered the scale. This lasted for a full ninety minutes, to when I made it back down to Medicine Rock for my usual sit. It was clearly a new vibratory peak, yet I was completely stable, present, immersed in bliss, and aware multi-dimensionally. I sat for another incredible thirty minutes in divine union, which I will briefly describe in a moment, before heading home. Now I was laughing aloud uncontrollably, and still crying of course! I would laugh like this for two solid hours, rolling around on the floor of my studio. I literally could not stop! At long last, likely due to reaching some physical limit, I settled into a vibrant humming stillness.

Now back to Medicine Rock. While this may be the most difficult thing to convey, it must at least be said. After all, this is an "awakening story." In the context of the flowering of consciousness, or of the human being realizing its true nature, this was the climax of the journey to date. My being would expand into a profound state of unity consciousness. It transcended everything, from the densest to the most subtle, yet included all of the magnificent diversity of life at every level. I was very much grounded in the physical, very much Gordon, and yet the "field" emanating from the spiritual heart was borderless and eternal. All of creation shared this quantum, divine, infinite center as a singular totality. I want to call this "full embodiment," not based on any accepted definition of the term, but because those are my best descriptive words. Of course, to use the word "full" would most surely be wrong. The exquisite mystery and incomprehensible nature of the awakening journey has taught me that. It often feels complete, but somehow never is.

As for this miraculous unfolding, it isn't enough to use phrases like "One with Christ" or having entered the "Kingdom of Heaven." These are truly profound communions and amazing divine states, but they still fall short in conveying this lived experience. There is still a beyond... a transcendent, empty, pregnant stillness... the very infinite womb of the Goddess. Everything in creation and potentiality is there, and yet so is that which is beyond it all. In full Union, there is no union that took place, for there is simply nothing to unite. One is not in Christ... one is Christ. One is not in the Kingdom of Heaven... one is the Kingdom. And through the miracle that is existence, one is the Universe walking around in the Universe. One is the embodiment of all the sacred Trinities... three in one and one in three. And above all, by the profound Grace of that single divine essence, one is also blissfully human.

Epilogue

TWO MONTHS HAVE passed since the ceremony. I have just finished writing Part Two of this book, which has been pouring out nonstop since I returned. It has been the all-consuming mission of the
moment... both beautiful and revelatory. I debated whether or not to
include the following story, as it is ultimately a superficial anecdote
and irrelevant to the larger narrative. However, it is thematically in
keeping with the unfolding of my personal story, so why not... a little
"crown" jewel.

This story took place in early June, shortly after I began documenting the Sedona mission. It would happen on a mountain hike
that was otherwise unremarkable, and featured no "mystical" events
of note. I was bounding up the hill, barefoot as usual, when I came to
a tree friend of mine that hangs across the trail at about chest height.
I always say hello as I duck under her, and have done so several
hundred times without incident. On this day, there would be one.
Due to nothing other than a lack of attention, I rose up prematurely
as I passed under the tree. She has a stub from where a branch had
broken off on the underside of her trunk. It was about three inches in
diameter and its end was a jagged ring of splintered wood that looked
like a round hairbrush. When I stood too quickly, I forcibly smashed
directly into the stub with the top of my head and sustained nearly
a dozen puncture wounds. It was sudden, bloody, and very painful!

I inspected and cleaned the wounds when I got home, revealing a well-defined circle... a "Medicine Wheel" of punctures on the
crown of my head. Given my interesting history with stigmata-themed

wounds, I had actually once wondered how one could possibly sustain multiple head puncture wounds without an actual crown of thorns... short of diving headlong into a cactus. Now I know! I had made it through Holy Week and thought my bizarre streak had come to an end, only to cut both hands and feet in Sedona. I figured that was that! Leave it to the Goddess to render me incredulous once more, and grace me with our own version of the ultimate crown. She knows me intimately well... and just what to get the man who already has everything, because he is Her servant. So blessed and loved am I.

Amen. Thank you. I love you.

Mystic Service Trinity Prayer

Beloved Father, who art Heaven
In gratitude we bow.
Thy Kingdom comes, Thy Will is done.
May I be an instrument of that holy Will.
Amen. Thank you. I love you.

Beloved Mother, full of Grace
The Lord is with thee.
Blessed art Thou, and blessed is the fruit of thy womb.
May I be both the fruit and the womb in holy service.
Amen. Thank you. I love you.

Beloved Brother, only begotten Son
Born one with the Father, by the power of the Holy Spirit.
May the living waters of Love flow through this
surrendered heart into God's holy Creation.
Amen. Thank you. I love you.